THE
FIVE
STAR
FEMALE
BOSS

★★★★★

Becoming a Manager Others Want to Follow

Alan E. Nelson, Ed.D.

Copyright © 2019 Alan E. Nelson

All rights reserved.

ISBN-9781701208650

Summit Publishing, Loveland, CO, USA

DEDICATION

This book is dedicated to our granddaughters, leaders from the future who will impact many lives. They will no doubt live in a world with more female bosses than anytime in history. Their Nanna (my wife) has been a truly amazing leader throughout her life, whether on John Maxwell's leadership team, or impacting the lives of 1000s of women in churches, or serving as an executive director for high-end senior living facilities. Women bring unique strengths to leading that are desperately needed in organizations. Heaven knows the world needs more Five-Star Female Bosses.

ACKNOWLEDGMENTS

I thank Andrea Zimmerman, who edited this book while being a mother, wife, editor, and amazing person.

I thank Karen Kluever and Thayer Riley as readers, smart women passionate about quality.

I thank Jeff White, a former colleague, brand guru, and graphic artist who designed this cover.

I thank Annette Zhang, an energetic intern who organized scores of studies and research related to new managers.

And as in most of my books, I thank my wife, Nancy, who's put up with my crap for over 38 years now. Her continual story-sharing and granular discussions of her work opportunities make these pages come to life, since most of my organizational leading is now in the rearview mirror. She's an amazing boss and life partner.

Table of Contents (TOC)

The cool thing about organizational behavior is that while topics are interrelated, they're not necessarily sequential. We've provided this order as a somewhat logical progression, so after the first couple of chapters, feel free to pick and choose. Check out this TOC and start with the topics that interest you the most. Hey, you're the boss, take charge of this book.

Introduction. Why Women Make Superior Leaders: While men dominated during the Industrial Age, the strengths women possess are aligned with organizations in the future. Their relational expertise lends itself to complex, cross-functional and socially savvy companies.

Chapter 1. Being in Charge: *Moving From Player to Coach:* Now that you're a boss, you need to think about managing people. Your main task is your team. The skills that got you to this place won't take you where you need to go. Nearly 60% of new managers never get trained, so this book is for you. (page 1)

Chapter 2. Eight Mistakes New Bosses Make: *To Avoid Pitfalls, You Must Know Where the Pits Are:* New bosses make common errors, resulting in over 50% of them washing out within their first year. If you want to avoid the pitfalls, you need to recognize the pits. Use this list to maneuver away from unnecessary mistakes. (page 7)

Chapter 3. Estimating Your Boss Aptitude: *Are You a Tall, Grande, or Venti?:* Are you wired to be a boss? Do you have what it takes? Just because someone gets a promotion doesn't mean he or she will succeed with a team. This is a tough but honest discussion of what it takes to lead and how to know if you have it. (page 15)

Chapter 4. The Boss Compass: *Navigating Between Leading & Managing Can Save Your Career:* Although we interchange these words, managing is significantly different from leading. Managing focuses primarily on the task and strives to maintain status quo with excellence. Leading focuses on people and strives to continually improve the organization. (page 21)

Chapter 5. The Supervision Continuum: *All Influence Is Not Created Equal:* All bosses are not the same. Influence varies from role to role and depends on how you're wired. This continuum compares entrepreneurs, transformational leaders, transactional leaders, managers, and administrators. (page 33)

Chapter 6. The Two Key Boss Qualities: *The DNA of Leadership Trust*: A significant number of studies show that what people want most in their bosses are competence and compassion. "Can we trust you?" and "Do you care about us?" Answer these correctly and you win. Answer them incorrectly and you lose. (page 39)

Chapter 7. Uber Thinking: *The DNA of Effective Decision-Making:* The critical thinking process focuses on identifying and distinguishing root from fruit problems, coming up with alternative solutions that include pros and cons, and then selects a solution along with mitigating risks and offering implementation ideas. (page 45)

Chapter 8. Decision-Making Blind Spots: *Avoiding Perception Biases:* This chapter defines 11 of the most common perception biases that impede effective decision-making by bosses and their teams. It includes a practical definition for identifying each and suggestions for avoiding them. (page 53)

Chapter 9. The C-Word: *The Boss's Kryptonite:* Change is the weak link in most leading. Over 70% of change efforts fail, so suggestions are provided for overcoming these failures, using the Nelson Change Model (NCM) that focuses on four factors: Leader Umph, Opinion Leader Readiness, Time, and Idea Impact. (page 63)

Chapter 10. SWOTting Your Org: *Analyzing Strengths, Weaknesses, Opportunities & Threats:* Your ability to discern your team and org's SWOT is a proven strategy to get a gist of an organization's health and standing. This chapter introduces the basics of a SWOT analysis so you can conduct one on your team, department, and company. (page 73)

Chapter 11. Social Banking: *The Power of Bartering Influence*: Exchanging social units to influence others is a vital skill among effective bosses. This chapter introduces social banking as a metaphor to understand what it takes to tap the influence ability of others, a key skill of effective leaders. (page 79)

Chapter 12. The Big Five: *Identifying Great Team Members:* This chapter introduces the most researched model of team member qualities, including conscientiousness, agreeableness, emotional stability, openness to new ideas, and extroversion. These all apply to leaders except for one. Can you guess which it is? (page 85)

Chapter 13. Motivational Strategies: *The Art & Science of Moving People:* This is the first part of two, introducing the more common motivational theories regarding employee engagement and performance. These offer unique insights for bosses to bring out the best in their people. (page 91)

Chapter 14. Motivational Strategies, Take 2: *More About Moving People:* This is the second part of two, introducing common motivational theories regarding employee engagement and performance. These offer additional insights for bosses to bring out the best in their people. (page 101)

Chapter 15. There's a U in Team: *Creating Synergy Among Your Members:* Developing your immediate team is your single most critical responsibility. Understand the 5-stage process of how teams evolve and gain practical ideas on how to increase cohesion. (page 109)

Chapter 16. Handling the Heat: *Managing Sparks w/o Burning Down the Office:* There's a difference between functional and dysfunctional conflict. This chapter introduces five styles for managing conflict, including collaboration, compromise, directing, accommodating, and avoidance. Each is effective in certain situations. (page 117)

Chapter 17. Competent Jerks: *& Other Team Members:* Every organization has them and sometimes they wind up on your team, talented people who bug everyone. This and three other types, based on performance and people skills, are defined. Developmental suggestions are included for each. (page 125)

Chapter 18. EI, EI, Oh!: *Farming Emotional Intelligence:* Emotional intelligence (EI) is a significant quality among Five-Star Bosses. EI is defined and illustrated, so that readers understand the 4-stage evolution along with the catalytic factor of motivation. No one enjoys working for a low EI manager. (page 131)

Chapter 19. Boss as Coach: *Basic Skills to Develop Your People:* This chapter introduces Socratic coaching, the skill set that focuses on developing people by asking strategic questions, not telling team members what to do. Ideas are provided for bosses to implement this tactic individually and in team settings. (page 139)

Chapter 20. Tapping Into Power: *Finding Influence in Interesting Places:* While most managers perceive power to be a position-oriented source, this chapter introduces six other sources that allow younger and less tenured bosses to improve their influence. These are offered with practical ideas on how to obtain them. (page 147)

Chapter 21. Badass Meetings: *How to Rock Your Gatherings:* Bosses are forever facilitating meetings, so best-practice ideas are provided to run more effective get-togethers. This avoids the waste of time and energy most meetings are accused of doing. (page 153)

Chapter 22. Bodacious Brainstorming: *Effective Ideation:* Basics in effective ideation, based on research-based methods for generating solutions, getting people to open up, avoiding dominators, and creating a healthy environment for non-judgmental discussions. (page 163)

Chapter 23. Sitch Leading: *Selecting the Style That Fits the Situation:* Situational leadership involves adapting the way you lead to the setting. These four styles are explained, along with practical ideas on how to match the appropriate styles to the conditions so you don't come across too strong or too weak. (page 173)

Chapter 24. Managing Expectations: *The Unwritten Law of Satisfaction:* Appeasing your boss and direct reports is not an easy task. One of the key skills of Five-Star Bosses is the proactive ability to manage the expectations of others, to avoid disappointing them and increasing tensions. (page 179)

Chapter 25. Work-Life Balance Myth: *Living in the Tension:* Advice is offered on getting the job done while not losing touch with family, friends, health, and avocations. Bosses have more responsibilities, so modeling this for your team members is important for their motivation as well. (page 189)

Chapter 26. Quick Picks: *Best-Practice Ideas You'll Find Helpful:* A variety of additional mini-themes, along with best-practice strategies, offer advice for new bosses. This section concludes with a list of un-edited comments from people surveyed on their frustrations with their bosses, to help you avoid these. (page 197)

Author Bio & Resources: Who in the world is this Alan E. Nelson, and what other books has he written that can enhance my leadership ability? (page 211)

Introduction

Why Women Make Superior Leaders

A Male Leadership Perspective

If someone asked you why women should be leaders, what would you say? If you responded, "Because they're long overdue," they might agree, but your argument would be unconvincing. If you answered, "Because women can lead as well as men," you'd also fail, because research shows that women must actually *outperform* men to be considered equal as leaders. If we're unable to effectively respond to this question, how do we hope to reduce the power gap between leaders who happen to be male and those who are female?

Over 39% of Fortune 1000 companies' workforce are women, but only 3% are CEO's, 14% executives and 16% board members (1). Even though 50% of US citizens are female, less than 20% make up Congress, and we've yet to see a woman VP or President. The list goes on in terms of power and pay differences, even though more women than men have graduated from college the last several years. Yet a recent study evaluating over 7000 leaders on effectiveness showed that women consistently outperformed men in 12 of the 15 roles measured. Jack Zenger concluded, "It is a well-known fact that women are underrepresented at senior levels of management. Yet the data suggests that by adding more women, the overall effectiveness of the leadership team would go up." (2)

After 30 years of studying organizational leadership, **I'm convinced of one thing: the world desperately needs more women leaders. I'm just as convinced that if women do not occupy more leadership roles in the future, we're doomed.** I've learned a lot about leadership since finishing my doctorate in the field in 1994. I've collected over 700 books on the topic, written nearly 200 articles, a dozen books, and over 150 hours of training curricula. I teach organizational behavior and performance and motivation at the University of Southern California's Marshall School of Business and am a Lecturer of Management at the Naval Postgraduate School. I have opportunities to teach some of the best and brightest up-and-coming students and military leaders in the world. But as I survey where organizations and society are headed, my fear is that we won't see sufficient numbers of females leading us into the future. This is not a male-authored intro on feminism or equality, but rather a lifelong student of leadership noting that the gender strengths of women are needed as organizations and society evolve.

Being married to a female leader for nearly 40 years, I'm familiar with the challenges women face. At 25, Nancy went on staff with leadership guru John Maxwell, a great mentor and leader himself. But over the years, she's experienced an array of subtle and overt struggles with chauvinistic organizations and environs. I recognize how women wrestle with being heard and taken seriously and thus gaining influence. But the tipping point of my conversion came after being invited to participate on a Navy research project regarding the integration of women into SEALs special forces. That research combined with my previous work of designing organizational training curricula for preteens and adolescents convinced me that we must focus our attention on young female leaders if the world is truly going to become a better place.

Women are uniquely gifted to lead in the 21st century. If we fail to understand and tap these unique gender strengths, organizations will grow increasingly sluggish and society as we know it will decay. Here are four primary reasons to promote women as leaders, not only for their sake, but for the sake of organizations and society at large.

Social experts: Women, in general, possess stronger relational strengths then men. The number of social interactions and relational connections they develop are significantly higher. You can see this in everyday life, by the way they converse with each other in cafes, waiting in line at the store, and measuring the length of their communications. Leaders are social architects. These soft-skills, requiring social-emotional intelligence, are typically found in greater abundance among socially astute individuals. The task-driven orientation of factories and production organizations lend themselves to male strengths. But as organizations become more multi-layered and process-driven, other skill sets are needed. The growing complexity of multi- national and cross-cultural communication means leaders must rely more on intuition, not just literal message content. High-contrast environs, where communication must be read nonverbally, lend themselves to the social strengths that women commonly possess.

Multi-dimensional: Women, in general, respond favorably to multi-tasking. We can see this in everyday life, in terms of how women commonly run the household, oversee child supervision, and work corporately. This ability to respond to a variety of potentially conflicting needs reflects what is required as organizations grow in complexity. While current CEO/President roles in organizations obligate multi-tasking, these conditions will increase and trickle down, such that those better able to tap both sides of the brain and "spin-plates" will offer superior leadership at all levels within an organization. This neurological disposition in women facilitates the busyness of business, without the overload that leads to poor decision making, frayed relations, and burnout.

Centric catalysts: Sally Helgesen noted in her book "The Female Advantage" that male-oriented organizations tend to be top-down, placing the leader in the highest box of the flow chart. Women, on the other hand, tend to lead from the middle, much like the hub of a wheel, with spokes emanating outward. This less hierarchical paradigm is more compatible with a world that functions increasingly democratically, with shared information and educated members. Centric-led versus top-down organizations catalyze idea sharing and communication, and tend to leave the leader less prone to the isolation that comes from the intimidation of position. This web-like leading style befits the flatter, more decentralized structure of organizations today that are likely to increase in the future.

Boundary spanning: This organizational behavior term refers to a team's willingness to go beyond its own borders. Because of the growing global village and sheer complexity of accomplishing goals, we must work with others outside of our team. The stereotypical scenario of the man never asking for directions represents the limitations of boundary spanning for males. Asking for help, reaching beyond our immediate turf, and integrating others is what is needed in the future. Women possess the strength of connecting with those outside of their immediate sphere of influence. Whether you're managing a Little League team in Scottsdale, Arizona or supervising an international project for a Fortune 500 company, the ability to connect with those outside of your immediate team is a strength that women bring to organizational culture. While this strength is relational in manner, it is unique in that it focuses on the ability to gain the expertise and leverage the network of those outside of one's own work group. Women are strategically poised to span boundaries as leaders, a skill that's required for both international as well as cross-team functions in today's and tomorrow's organizational complexities.

Carpe Diem

So how can female leaders take advantage of the current and emerging environment where their strengths will be embraced? Seize opportunities: Research shows that women often receive fewer promotions because they do not go after new experiences to demonstrate their abilities. They seem less likely to embrace new opportunities than men because they feel the need to be confident that they'll be able to handle the new challenge (90-100% sure), whereas men take it on with a much lower threshold (50-60% sure). The result is that men accept the project and promotion and for the most part, benefit from seizing the moment. Since women are slightly more risk-averse than men, they pass up opportunities that can elevate them in the organization and demonstrate their strengths and abilities. If you see a project or promotion that interests you, but don't feel confident that you can succeed at it, take it anyway. Chances are the fact it interests you shows that you have much of what it takes to succeed, and the actual experience will afford the opportunity for you to learn what you lack and to make up the difference.

Create coalitions: There is strength in numbers. A team outperforms an individual in most situations. Therefore, women benefit from the power of a "tribe." Team builders are more in demand today than ever before and will continue to be in the future. Whether it's a formal work team focusing on a project or an informal team you put together for breakfast, lunch, or happy hour socializing, gaining lateral allies gives you OPI (other people's influence). Lone Rangers get squashed, especially when you're a Lone Female Leader, so who can you reach out to (male and female) for the purpose of creating both social- and task-oriented teams? Take a portion of your daily routine to keep in touch with your coalition members. Make it a part of your weekly agenda. Even though it may appear more social and less formal, these informal networks empower those who are known and liked.

Network strategically: The irony is that while women possess a unique strength in socializing and relationship, the research shows that men are more strategic in how they ply their social wares. In other words, they go after friendships that can leverage their careers, either by opening doors of opportunities, riding coattails, or offering wisdom. Most jobs are obtained through who we know, not online job boards. You learn from what you do, but you get an opportunity to do those things based on who you know.

Strategic networking is different from creating a coalition in that it focuses more on individuals and power and influence. Ask a person you respect to mentor or sponsor you. Learn from them. Do you get invited to the meeting before the meeting? Do you see people gathering in a room and you wonder, why wasn't I invited to that? If not, chances are you've not done your work on the political side of strategic networking. Granted, some of this may be challenging if it takes place on the golf course, local pub, or after work hours, but figure out who you need to use your relational abilities with and who might help you learn and move up the ladder.

ID and Develop Young Leaders*: Perhaps the most powerful tool you have as a woman leader is to raise up other leaders. Think higher math. Talent adds to an organization; leading followers multiplies, but leading leaders produces exponential payoff. Most of the women leaders I've met seem preoccupied with their own responsibilities as well as juggling social roles (wife, mother), leaving little bandwidth to invest in next-gen female leaders. This is unfortunate, because no one understands the unique challenges of leading as a woman than another woman. Maintaining margin for opportunities to mentor and train preteens, teens, and 20-somethings is an important give-back that most women leaders overlook, because they're so focused on organizational responsibilities and spinning plates of family, friends, and private time. "What I Wish I'd Known About Leadership" is a narrative book we wrote, focusing on an experienced leader sharing wisdom with a protégé. Women leaders need to assess girls/teens with an aptitude for leading, because focusing on next-gen leaders is the best strategy for creating a critical mass of women leaders. Following is the rationale.

Why Young?

Accumulated experience: According to a blog published by Harvard Business Review, a survey of over 17,000 managers denoted that the first formal leadership training takes place at 42 years of age.[2] That's decades past the time when character is still malleable and cognitions are elevated, while still unencumbered by bad habits and negative experiences created over time. In addition, imagine the effect of compounding years of leading and 100s of training opportunities. Malcolm Gladwell, in his book "Outliers," explains the research behind those who achieve greatly and the amount of practice sessions that take place prior. If we wait until 40 or even 30 to begin serious leadership training, we've lost other strategic windows of developmental opportunity, not to mention needing to unlearn bad habits.

There are youth programs that supposedly develop leaders, but why aren't they producing the quantity and quality of leaders needed today? What about ASB (student government), Girl Scouts, National Charity League, Interact, Rotaract, 4-H, and any number of wonderful organizations that claim to offer leadership training? The problem is that nearly all of the preteen, teen, and early adult training programs called leadership that we've reviewed actually have little to do with specific leadership skills. If you compared and contrasted high-end executive training programs with youth "leadership" programs, you'd find few similarities. The latter involve good citizenship—beneficial for everyone—but they don't distinguish what leaders specifically *do*. Self-esteem, confidence, character, and service are all wonderful qualities. We want them in our leaders, but they do not distinguish what makes leaders different from others.

Leadership is the process of helping people accomplish together what they would not or could not as individuals. Leaders are those who get leadership going. Most cultures don't consider leadership an adolescent behavior. Kids hear "Someday you'll be a leader." Few women have experienced executive- caliber leadership training, and fewer still have learned how to deliver it to others. The result is that what so many think is leadership training is really little more than opportunities for personal growth and occasional venues for leading (without specific instruction), coaching, and feedback. The idea that "everyone can be a leader" reflects a definition that leading is being a responsible, self-actualized individual. While we want leaders to emulate good-citizen qualities, these qualities do not distinguish how to get people to follow you. There is a difference between being a leader and leading people.

Women nurturers: Walk into any elementary school and you'll see a vast majority of women teachers. The reason is that women, in general, are the nurturers in families and society. That natural bond between females and other young females offers significant potential for women leaders to mentor young women leaders. No one can mentor women leaders like other women leaders. To begin with, the sexual awkwardness of men serving as sponsors and mentors of dynamic female protegees lends itself to all sorts of challenges. But just as important is that women who are leaders understand what it is to be young, female, and influentially oriented. While leaders can develop other leaders to a point, men possess sufficient differences to limit effective mentoring of women. Just as speaking the same language is important to effective teaching, gender language differences make it difficult for opposite sexes to sufficiently mentor one another.

Ethically moldable: Leaders must deal in power. A powerless leader is an oxymoron. The problem is that power tempts us to do things we normally would not, resulting in selfish ambition and any number of corrupt behaviors, often hurting people and bankrupting organizations. Moral psychologists suggest that our character is primarily established by early- to mid-teens. While we can change after that point, it comes with difficulty and much intentional effort. Therefore, if we want ethical leaders, we need to get to them long before their MBA course in ethics. While ethical parenting is important, ethical leadership training is even more imperative, because leaders must deal in shades of gray and benefit from understanding how their decisions impact a team and organizational outcomes. Thus, identifying leaders at a very young age and recruiting them into an ethical leadership training program intensifies the chances of raising effective and ethical leaders.

Critical mass: Growing leaders is in some ways similar to growing food. Throughout history and until 200 years ago, we cultivated gardens in small lots. Then, thanks to the technology of tractors and small equipment, we increased our productivity. The average farm grew from an acre or two to several hundred acres. But a few decades ago, we evolved from farms to ag business, creating virtual food factories of 1000s of acres. For the most part, leadership development is precariously perched between the garden and farm eras. But this approach will require centuries for us to significantly grow more female leaders.

If we hope to create a critical mass of women leaders, we must create a training pedagogy that can systematically identify and develop hundreds of thousands of young female leaders, through the use of powerful, accelerated learning methods. A training curriculum called SheLead, using project-based learning with feedback and coaching was recently developed to address that gap. Designed after executive-caliber training, the program stimulates significant growth among the top 10-20% with leadership aptitude, from ages 10 and up.

The world desperately needs more and better women leaders because the organizations of the future will require the unique gender strengths that women possess. The authors of *The Athena Doctrine* noted in their research that if male leaders want to be effective in the future, they'll need to adopt many of these traits considered feminine. Once again, research points toward female strengths being in greater demand among leaders, now as well as in the future. (3) Finally, there really is a female advantage in leadership; perhaps there always was, but we just didn't recognize it. Hopefully we'll develop sufficient quantities of women leaders to fill the needs. But unless we begin doing things differently, that won't happen. **If you want to improve the world, focus on women leaders. If you want to improve women leaders, focus on them while they're young.**

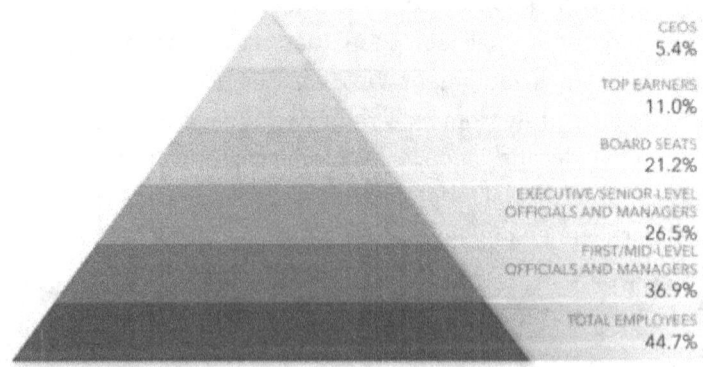

WOMEN IN S&P 500 COMPANIES

(4)

1. "A Study in Leadership" by Zenger/Folkman, 2012.
2. HBR Blog Network, "We wait too long to train leaders," Jack Zenger, Dec. 17, 2012.
3. *The Athena Doctrine* by John Gerzema & Michael D'Antonio, SF, 2013.
4. Retrieved from www.Catalyst.org October 19, 2019

Chapter 1
Being in Charge
Moving From Player to Coach

What Got You Here Won't Get You There

We're all familiar with the concepts of five-star generals, five-star hotels and restaurants, and even five-star Uber drivers. It would seem we critique the quality of everything today. So how would you rate the bosses you've had? How would you rate yourself as a boss? Who wouldn't like their direct reports to give them five stars? So what does it take to become a Five-Star Boss?

Welcome to my book, which is your book now. And since it is primarily written for those who've been promoted and/or hired as a new boss, congratulations may be in order! Whether you're the assistant manager of a local pizza restaurant or a freshly minted project director of a multinational corporation, you've entered a different arena. Chances are you've been a great player on the field, but now you're a coach. Even if you're a player coach, overseeing a team is a unique venture. Unfortunately, nearly half of all new managers wash out within the first year. That's not only a detriment to the organizations they serve but also an incredible disappointment to those who don't cut it in their new roles. Plus it irritates the dickens out of those who report to these bosses.

A primary reason is a lack of training. One study showed that nearly 60% of new bosses never get trained on how to manage. That's a big mistake, because what makes you a good salesperson isn't what makes you good at overseeing salespeople. What makes you a great pizza maker isn't what makes you a great team leader of pizza makers. You get the point: skills that got you here won't take you there. Organizations in all industries are notorious for promoting people with strong technical skills and elevating them to be in charge of people without thinking through if that person has the capacity to do this, and if so, how to train them for this different skill set.

Who Should Read This Book

Over the years, I've been a student of leadership. As a 10-year-old in school, my fellow classmates would come up to me at recess and ask what we should play. I'd pick soccer, or softball, or Red Rover, but never thought of myself as a leader. You'd have thought my teachers would appreciate my ability, but instead I got a few C's in conduct—primarily because I was a bit of a class clown and tended to steal the attention of my colleagues away from the teacher. Now, my primary research since 2008 has involved the study of young leader emergence, primarily for those between ages 10 and 18 but including 3- to 23-year-olds as well.

The purpose of this book is also about emerging leaders, but older ones.

I've had the opportunity to teach leadership at some wonderful institutions, including Pepperdine University, the Naval Postgraduate School, USC Marshall School of Business, and the University of California Irvine Merage School of Business. A large majority of my students plan to be a boss, have been identified by superiors as up-and-coming leaders, or are currently managers. In addition, I've worked with small, medium, and multibillion-dollar companies who've consistently admitted, year after year, that one of their biggest pain points is finding competent new managers.

Therefore, this book is dedicated to them, the new bosses of companies, military, public agencies, and non-profits. Leadership is one of the most desirable qualities because for the most part, leaders make more money, possess more power, and enjoy work and life more than others. But at the end of the day, everyone isn't cut out to be a leader. Nearly all of us have experienced a teacher, boss, CEO, or supervisor who, well, wasn't very good at managing others. You don't want to be one of those people, do you?

Another group of people reading this book may be "management," the individuals who run organizations and are looking for the next high potential, successor, or team leader. As I said, the traditional way that society elevates new managers is broken and thus, dysfunctional. This book will help you identify skill sets for developing your new bosses along with what to look for in emerging leaders before you promote an employee to a managerial role. A recent Gallup study noted that the most important single key to an organization's success is the manager. This book is a primer for your new bosses.

A third group this book may benefit are the bosses who aren't new but may be stuck, whether they realize it or not. Let's be honest, the research says that leaders typically rank themselves higher than their followers rank them. We humans in general tend to overestimate ourselves. For example, 96% of people think they're above average in people skills. If average is 50%, then, well, we have some distortion of reality. If you're an experienced but plateaued manager, this book can revitalize your thinking and help you brush up on the essentials. The best athletes go back to the basics when they're in a slump or want to take their skills to the next level.

People Don't Quit Jobs—They Quit Bosses

Employee turnover costs organizations a significant amount of money, not to mention intangibles such as demotivation, stress, and workload management. What's the main reason people quit their job? Is it low pay? Long commute? Incongruence with org culture? No, no, and no. Over 80% of people who quit their jobs state it is primarily because they don't like their bosses. People don't quit their jobs; they quit their bosses. By now you probably understand this statistic, because chances are you've had a bad boss or two. There's nothing that sucks the joy from a job more than having to deal with a difficult boss. But that's good news for you, because it takes so little to be above average. And if you're motivated to be above average, even exceptional, the marketplace is ready for you.

So while the world is filled with opportunities for Five-Star Bosses, the problem is that being in charge is not easy. If it were, we wouldn't be screaming for more and better leaders. Although I'll be talking about the differences between leading and managing, for now I'm interchanging the terms boss, manager, and leader. I'm doing this in part because these terms are commonly interchanged in organizations today, and when you're a boss, you need to be able to both lead and manage and discern when each skill set is needed.

As you can tell by now, this book isn't going to be a stuffy, academic text. I'll sometimes use a casual, coffee-chat style to help you embrace the content as if you were hanging out with a favorite mentor or college prof. Yet don't confuse the casual nature of the writing with shooting-the-breeze. I get to meet some very bright students, highly motivated and driven. These include NASA engineers, Navy SEALs, fighter jet pilots, spies, and an occasional retired rear admiral and national leader offspring. I teach courses on leadership, organizational change, human capital performance and motivation, and such. These are research-based, utilizing well-respected texts and articles and Harvard Business School case studies. After nearly 40 years of leading and learning and listening, I'd like to share what I've learned that will help you as a new boss make the most of your opportunity.

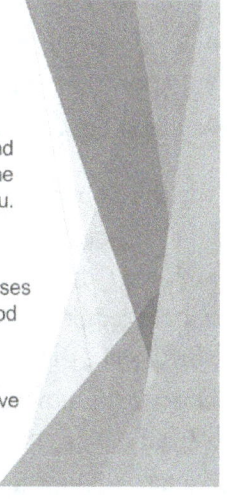

Digestion Suggestions

The Five-Star Boss is a collage of organizational behavior and leadership themes, taught in top business schools. Peruse the chapter topics and decide which seem most interesting to you. Feel free to read these first. They're ordered in a somewhat logical pattern, but are not sequential.

This book focuses on the more common issues plaguing bosses and frustrating their direct reports. That's what makes it a good primer for those newer to managing.

Also check out the author's Five-Star Boss podcast series at https://thenelsons.podbean.com. Dr. Nelson is available for live training.

Make Your Choice

When asked to be a boss, people should make one of three choices.

The first option is to graciously resign. That's right, I said "graciously resign." The reason is that management isn't for everyone. Some people find that it's out of their gift mix and just don't enjoy it. In spite of the added pay and freedom, it creates more of a burden than it's worth. If you love technical skills and more hands-on work with your peers, then you're probably better off not being in charge. This doesn't mean you're not smart, motivated, or competent. It just means you know who you are and it's not a good fit. By graciously resigning, you're saying "Thanks so much for believing in me, but 'no thanks,' I'll stick to what I know I'm good at." This will save you and others a lot of unpleasant experiences as well as time.

The second option is to be mediocre. "I want to be average!" That's right, mediocrity is the result of not being good at something. The average boss hasn't trained or prepared to be a boss, so he or she isn't good at it. This doesn't make them a bad person, just not a very good boss. The reason is either people didn't graciously turn down the job or they tried to do the same thing they did in their previous role, or, God forbid, they mimicked what they've seen other mediocre bosses do. I understand that sometimes you don't know what you're good at and enjoy until you try it, so there's no harm in test-driving a new position. But know that at the end of the day, being a boss may not be what you're cut out to do. If it is, you need to get a new game plan.

The third option is to change gears, to retrain your brain how you think about who you are and how you accomplish your job. This is what is required from excelling as a player to succeeding as a coach. Managing people requires a different skill set than managing tasks and projects. That's what this book is about, describing what is required to be effective as a manager, not mediocre. The opportunity you have now is a great one, so if you don't want to choose options one and two, you'll need to change gears. At the end of the day, you still may decide to graciously resign, but at least you'll have given it a fair chance. You don't need to be embarrassed by that decision. There are more things in life we're not wired to do than we are. But you may be one those people who truly are created to lead others and you'll be stepping into your potential. You'll make people happy, continue to get promoted, and find fulfillment in your role. That's the motivation behind this book.

Five-Star Boss Questions:

1. Why are you reading this book?
2. What do you want to get out of it?
3. What are two or three things you think you're doing well as a boss?
4. What are two or three things you want to grow in as a boss?
5. As you look at the Table of Contents, which chapters intrigue you the most?

Chapter 2

Eight Mistakes New Bosses Make

*To Avoid Pitfalls,
You Must Know Where the Pits Are*

Don't Be That Boss

On January 1, 1929, not far from where I live, a momentous sporting event took place with a surprising play that would go down in history. The Golden Bears played the Georgia Tech Yellow Jackets in the Rose Bowl. Roy Riegels, an All-American for the Bears, picked up a fumble just 30 yards from the Yellow Jackets' end zone. But during the play, Riegels got turned around and began running toward the opponent's goal line. When he was 3 yards from scoring a touchdown for the Yellow Jackets, his own quarterback tackled him. The ball was placed at the 1-yard line. The Bears chose to punt but it was blocked, leading to a safety and giving Georgia Tech 2 points that allowed them to win, 8-7. "Wrong Way

Riegels" went down in infamy as a talented player who bungled a great opportunity.

Although they might not be as famous (or infamous), countless talented people make similar mistakes as they begin their roles as a boss. Most are intelligent, dedicated employees who demonstrate stellar technical skills. But in the role of boss, they bungle the play and let down their team. Here are eight of the most common errors new bosses make. The purpose of this list is to pre-warn you about frequent issues. It sets the course for what the rest of the book will strive to remedy, but offers a succinct overview of the most frequent mishaps of new bosses.

1. *Thinking automatic, not manual*: If you go into your new role as a boss with the mindset you had in your previous role, you're in for a bumpy road. It's like trying to drive a stick shift (manual) vehicle the way you do an automatic. Typically, people who get promoted to managerial roles have shown expertise in some other area, usually in a more technical and detailed task. Any number of reasons can be behind the promotion, but often what got the person to the role of being in charge won't make him or her good at managing. "What got you here won't take you there." This book is about making the paradigm shift from overseeing tasks and projects to overseeing teams and people. If you don't make the shift in your thinking, you'll be far less effective than you've been in the past, disappointing you and the organization you serve.

2. *Confusing power with control:* Now that you possess more power, don't try to control too much. No one enjoys being micro-managed, having the boss staring over them as they work, continually interrupting to correct, reprove, or just observe. So, although people don't like it as a team member, they often do that when they become the team leader. Much of it has to do with failing to change one's mindset. They can't seem to let go of being a doer versus an overseer. Bosses must delegate tasks to team members and empower them. That requires trust. If you don't trust the capabilities of your team

members, then as the boss you need to make sure they get trained and motivated. This is not accomplished by micromanaging. Let your people do their work. Check in and hold them accountable, but get out of their way.

3. *Confusing being the boss with being bossy*: Something very odd happens when you give a person a title as manager, team leader, shift leader, or boss. Many people think they must become bossy. They begin ordering people around, telling them what to do, and nit-picking over things that would drive them nuts when they were a team member. The main reason for bossy bosses is that this is what they've seen from previous bosses. We pass on the dysfunction from generation to generation of supervisors. Five-Star bosses aren't bossy. They don't bark commands to their team members. Rather, they lead by example, encouragement, and training. These require more work in the long run, which is another reason people become bossy... laziness.

5-Star Bosses Reduce Their Ignorance

The only victories that leave no regret are those gained over ignorance. -Napoleon Bonaparte

Ignorance, the root and stem of all evil. -Plato

Being ignorant is not so much a shame as being unwilling to learn. -Benjamin Franklin

Nothing is more terrible than to see ignorance in action. -Johann Wolfgang von Goethe

I am not ashamed to confess, I am ignorant of what I do not know. -Cicero

Ignorance is never out of style. It is in fashion today, it is the rage today, and it will set the pace tomorrow. -Frank Dane

4. *THE task isn't YOUR task*: Some organizations promote people to full-time managerial roles, while others are in hybrid roles of part-time team member and part-time team leader. Regardless, managers are in charge of people, not just projects. If you become overly task-oriented, your people problems will

accumulate. When that happens, task accomplishment slows and now you're behind in both areas. *The task of the leader is the team. The task of the team is the task.* Let me say that again, in case it didn't soak in, "The task of the LEADER is the TEAM. The task of the TEAM is the TASK." Keeping that in mind helps you look up from being a doer to becoming a people mover. When team members feel like they're just parts of a machine you're running, that they're being used, they'll be less motivated and you'll be less effective in your role. This is counterintuitive to many who were so effective at project completion.

5. *Sophomoric thinking:* As a professor, sometimes I like to have fun with my undergrad students. I'll ask, "How many of you are freshmen?" Then I'll ask, "How many of you are sophomores? Do you know the etymology for the word "sophomore"? It's from two Greek words: *sophos*, where we get our word 'sophistication,' and *moros*, where we get our word 'moron.' So literally, a sophomore is a sophisticated moron." (Insert awkward laughter.) It makes sense because we know freshmen are morons, meaning they don't know a lot, but after a year, students begin thinking they know more than they do. Second-year students often look down at their immature counterparts, only a year their junior. So while they're more sophisticated than they used to be, they still don't know a lot. So what's my point?

A common feeling among newer (and sometimes older) bosses is that they are expected to be the smartest person in the room. Henry Ford said that he hired people smarter than him...don't assume that you should know how to do everything. If you don't feel comfortable going to your supervisor for ideas, then find a colleague, a friend with managerial experience, or someone in your company you can trust who is wise and experienced. People who try to act smart, but don't learn, end up losing credibility and thus diminishing their influence. Later in the book we'll talk about finding a mentor, but advice-seeking is more about specifics. It could be asking about policy, protocol, and politics. When you're a new boss, you're like the new kid at school. It may feel embarrassing to ask "newbie" questions (how do I log in to the copy machine or fill out a purchase order or submit a credit card receipt), but don't apologize. Ask what you need to know and quickly identify who your go-to person is for need-to-know information. This too is a good issue to ask about. Try to avoid sophomoric thinking.

6. *Tripping up the stairs:* Most managers are sandwiched between having a boss and being a boss. That's a precarious position. Your effectiveness is based on your ability to lead your team as well as help your supervisor be more productive. If you don't understand your boss's communication style, priorities, and what his/her supervisor's goals are, then you're going to stumble in meeting expectations. That's what I call "tripping up the stairs." Later on, we'll talk about 360-degree leading (up, down, and laterally), but for now, know that for you to be a good boss, you need to "have your boss's back." To better understand how he or she thinks, ask others who report to your boss about what's important to that person and even about little things like pet peeves. Figure out how he or she is wired, and do your best to sincerely serve without appearing to "brown nose," kiss up, or suck up... okay, you get it. Only weak-ego people appreciate such behavior, and if your boss is wired that way, you're going to have many other issues to deal with.

7. *The Mirror Syndrome:* Remember the evil queen in Snow White? "Mirror, mirror on the wall, who's the fairest of them all?" The insecure power-wielder depended on something else for her strokes; she needed to be liked. That's a temptation for leaders too, because hey, we're human. If you're managing a team different from the one you used to be on, it will be easier than trying to be in charge of people who were your colleagues and even friends. If you do end up managing your previous team, it may be best to have one-on-one, honest discussions with how appreciative you are to have the new role and how

awkward it feels to be in charge. Depending on the situation, there may be some feelings of jealousy that they didn't get selected or even disrespect that now you're "one of *them*." You may need to draw some lines in the sand and establish boundaries, while still maintaining a humble attitude. We'll talk more about the challenges of hitting the right balance of moving from buddy to boss.

8. *BIZAU:* I enjoy trying to figure out personalized license plates. Some people get very creative, and others simply create private acronyms. A lot of new bosses drive around with BIZAU on their vehicles, meaning business as usual. When you're new, you have a fine line to walk. You don't want to come in like a raging bull, turning things over and making a lot of changes. Yet a more typical misstep is doing little to nothing differently. Being new offers a unique opportunity to make some changes that people will allow because "she doesn't know any better." This is what we call short-term credit. Leaders typically must earn the right to make changes, but new bosses can take advantage of this new phase. If you don't do anything new, people are going to assume that you're a status quo monger, and any change you attempt in the future will be more difficult. Understand this primarily pertains to your area of responsibility. If you begin speaking up in meetings with your boss or colleagues and start making suggestions from your previous job, you'll irritate others. Take a while in these settings to listen, build rapport, and get a lay of the land so that you don't sound naïve. Understanding context is important for new bosses; it helps you learn where the landmines are hidden and how to avoid stepping on them. Figure out small things you can do initially to make a few changes, testing to see how open others are to change. You want others to see that this won't be business as usual.

This list varies from boss to boss, but these items tend to be the ones you hear a lot about, both from supervisors as well as team members. Having them on your radar is important because you want to be self-aware in your new role, without becoming paranoid. The rest of the book will touch on all of these issues in more detail and how to avoid them, along with several other best-practice themes.

Five-Star Boss Questions:

1. What other items would you add to this list that you've experienced in observing new bosses?
2. Of this list, which would seem to be the top three that you're more vulnerable to and/or likely to commit?
3. What are a few things you could do to be more diligent in avoiding these missteps?
4. Of this list, which two would seem to be at the bottom of your list, based on what you know about yourself and the context of your role?
5. What is one thing you know you don't know that you want to learn about?

Chapter 3
Estimating Your Boss Aptitude

Are You a Tall, Grande, or Venti?

Capacity vs. Activation

I'm a big Starbucks fan. In fact, much of this book was written in Starbucks stores. My go-to drink is a Grande dark roast with 2.5 packets of Splenda and some 2% milk. Even though I don't drink black coffee, I never ask "for room." The reason is that if you ask for room, many if not most baristas leave ¾ of an inch of empty space at the top. When I'm spending $20 per gallon for java, I'm not about to leave empty space. If it's too full, I spill a little into the trash (like a lot of customers) and then do my recipe. A Tall is 12 ounces, a Grande 16, and a Venti holds 20. Here's my point: when I order a Grande, I want all 16 ounces. I don't want it 80% or 90% filled. But even at the brim, I'm not going to get more than a pint of Joe. So when it comes to leading, what's your capacity? Are you a Tall, Grande, or Venti?

No matter how much capacity you possess for leading, you'll want to maximize your potential. Living otherwise is a waste. Can a person change his/her potential, or merely realize it? No one knows. Some things such as IQ are like eye color and hair—not apt to change much. We're born with certain capacities. As you look at what we're learning from genetic science, between 10% and 60% of leadership wiring is hereditary, depending on what quality you're analyzing. Thus, I'm of the school that believes we're born with a basic wiring or capacity for leading. The questions become, how do we estimate a person's capacity and then how do we best develop it? Given the analogy of the Starbucks cups, a full Tall will outperform a half-full Venti. What a waste of the Venti. But if an organization needs Venti leadership, it's unfair to recruit Tall or Grande leaders because we're setting them up to fail. That's unfortunate for the organization and the leaders.

Someone said, "Anyone can count the seeds in an apple, but only God can count the apples in a seed." That's sort of what humans strive to do as we analyze a person's capacity within a given role or field, whether it's academics, athletics, arts, or leadership. So let's briefly look at some things pertinent to estimating leadership capacity in ourselves and others.

Type I & Type II Leader Qualities

Leaders are born and built. As with the other domains of giftedness, we can't specify what amounts of nature and nurture exist, but we need to realize that both come into play when predicting an individual's efficacy. As I mentioned, a growing amount of research in the field of neuroscience indicates that a certain percent of leadership aptitude is genetic. The problem is that most leadership assessments focus on efficacy (what makes a leader effective) rather than emergence (who's most likely to emerge as a leader). The former analyzes people already in leadership roles, as opposed to those most likely to succeed if recruited.

If we want to assess leadership capacity and gifting, we need to focus on what is unique to leading. Most inventories confuse qualities we seek in leaders with what distinguishes those who lead from non-leaders. For example, people agree that leaders should be good listeners, because hearing out team members harvests ideas, improves trust, and engenders commitment. But good listening is also a skill we value in all team members, not just in those who lead. Therefore, listening does not distinguish what leaders do from non-leaders. Conversely, the ability to convene people, gathering them to work on a shared goal, is something that distinguishes leaders from non-leaders. The former characteristic is what we may call a Type II quality, something we want our leaders to have but doesn't distinguish what leaders do uniquely from others. The latter quality is a Type I characteristic, something that differentiates leaders from others (below). Another way of saying it is, *Type I qualities make people leaders; Type II qualities make them more effective.*

Non-essential Qualities (Type II)   **Essential Qualities (Type I)**

Qualities we seek in strong people

Qualities we seek in leaders

If you review a number of leadership assessments, you'll notice that 80-100% use Type II qualities. If you're offering a 360-assessment on a leader to target areas for improvement, these types of questions make more sense. Frequently, "What do you like most in a leader?" surveys prompt researchers to look at the qualities people desire in their bosses as opposed to what actually makes leadership happen. Type II characteristics improve leader efficacy, but they're secondary when you're trying to figure out who possesses a larger capacity to lead. Identification of giftedness is different from skill improvement.

Type I Leader Qualities (NYLI)	Type II Leader Qualities
• P1. Persuasive: the ability to get others to see things differently and buy into your ideas and vision • P2. Propelled: internal locus of control, efficacy, achievement-oriented inspiring others to persevere • P3. Planner: comfortable with abstract thinking, can come up with ideas and assign tasks that others accept • P4. Power: exudes boldness, courage, and confidence that impresses others to notice and follow	• 21st Century Skills • Critical thinker / decisive • Collaborative / relational • Creative / curious • Communicates / listens • Confident / high self-esteem • Humble / open-minded • Moral / ethical • Positive / hopeful • Charismatic / likeable • Smart / intelligent • Flexible / adaptable

Examples of Type I (Essential) and Type II (Non-essential) Leader Qualities

My work since 2008 has primarily focused on identifying Type I leadership qualities, reflecting giftedness. Our work has involved thousands of 10- to 18-year-olds globally, as well as reviewing research regarding adult leadership. Type I leadership qualities consist of four primary characteristics, all of which need to be present. For more info, contact us for a free white paper on the subject.

Essential Qualities

By focusing on the must-have qualities required for leading, you avoid two common errors: false positives and confusing correlation with cause-and-effect. When too many Type II qualities are used in formal and informal inventories, you often identify individuals with charming personalities who are likable and have people skills, but when asked to organize others, can't. Although these preceding qualities are common among effective leaders, they are not essential for leading. Thus, when a person with these qualities is promoted to a role where leading is expected, you often don't see it. "Hey John, why don't you head up the company-wide annual holiday event?" The person's eyes glaze over and resemble your computer screen, buffering a large file that won't download.

So while we see a number of Type II characteristics evident in effective leaders, many of these would also be present in highly functioning, self-actualized individuals who are ineffective at leading. Can these characteristics help a leader be more effective? They can, which is why they are often included in 360-improvement instruments, but they don't *cause* leading. They're also evident in people who do not lead. This is why in organizational life, we often recruit, promote, and hire individuals who appear to be leaders we've seen, but they fail miserably because they do not possess the ability to lead an organization. I refer to this as "The O Factor." (For more info on this topic as it relates to 3- to 23-year-olds, please read my book *The O Factor*.)

Just because a person is smart, good with others, charismatic, and ethical or has occupied a position of supervision in the past, doesn't mean s/he can lead. Many of these characteristics correlate with good leading, but they don't cause the effect we seek, creating frustration for everyone and making us wonder what went wrong in the process. We've created a free, online assessment that adults can do on 6- to 18-year-olds. An adult version of this exists, titled New Manager Inventory (NMI). You can find this at my website: www.AlanENelson.com.

Determining a good estimate of your leadership capacity is important in avoiding the Peter Principle, a concept developed by Laurence J. Peter that notes how people in a hierarchy rise to their level of incompetence. An employee is promoted based on his success in previous jobs until he reaches a level at which he is no longer competent. Probably, over the course of your career, you've met quite a few people whose job performance seems to be explained by this principle. Proficiency in one skill set doesn't equate with success in another. While we never want to minimize the potential of an individual, it's best to apply ourselves where we're apt to succeed, based on our potential. Sometimes we don't know that until we accept a position that we're ill-equipped for success in, but to do this over and over is both a disservice to the employee and the organization.

Five-Star Boss Questions:

1. Think of an example of a leader you're familiar with who seemed to have a lot of potential as a leader but never developed it. What happened?
2. What do you think your leadership potential is, and how well is it developed?
3. Describe a child or youth you know who seems to exude a lot of natural leadership ability. What are the indicators you noticed?
4. Take the NMI assessment and/or have someone else do it on you. This can be found at www.AlanENelson.com and follow the links to the online instrument. (It's free.)
5. What can you do to enhance your leadership skills (in addition to finishing this book)?

Chapter 4

The Boss Compass

Navigating Between Leading & Managing Can Save Your Career

Kissing Cousins, NOT Identical Twins

Get ready, because I'm going to mess with your head a bit. Do you want to be a manager, or do you want to be a leader? What's the difference? Most people think of them as the same. In certain circles, the two words are used interchangeably. That's probably because most companies don't use "leader" as a job title, instead using executive titles (Chief Executive Officer, President, Chief Financial Officer) to denote company leadership and upper management. But most of us who study organizational life separate the two words because they each mean something different. So hang in there with me as I offer some distinctions.

Let's say you have a pick-up truck and a passenger car. Both of these are vehicles. Both are drivable, but they typically differ in terms of whether you're hauling cargo or passengers. In this word picture, managing is more like a pick-up and leadership is more like a car. We manage tasks and lead people. So if you're focusing on a task or situation with people, you'll typically want to use your pick-up truck. If you're dealing with conflict or offering a vision-cast, bring the car. I know it's a matter of nuance and certainly the processes overlap, but it's important to establish a difference because it will help you better understand when you need to lead and when you should be managing. They are very complementary, yet very different, processes. They're more like close-knit cousins, each with family resemblances but with unique personalities and looks.

Defining Leadership

Let me drive a stake in the ground of how I define leadership. At one time I had over 700 books on leadership in my library. Yet after reading or reviewing them all, barely 5% offered any significant definition of the term. So while everyone likes to talk about leading, the term is used a lot of different ways, including self-motivation, acting as a good citizen, and personal drive—nothing that deals with helping others to accomplish goals together. Because it sells well and everyone likes to think of themselves as a leader, we put this word on many products and services that have little to nothing to do with actual leading.

Leadership is an interesting word. The term didn't appear in English literature until the early 1800s. Isn't that amazing? Obviously, leaders have existed throughout history and people have been in awe of those who lead, but the term itself is relatively modern. In the past, we've focused on leaders. What do leaders do? They lead. But "leadership" is the social process of helping people accomplish together what they would not or could not as individuals.

> **Leadership** is the process of helping people accomplish together what they would not or could not as individuals.
>
> **Leaders** are individuals who catalyze this process.
>
> **Leading** is how they do it.

Based on our use of these terms, leadership is a social process. It involves motivating others (*what they would not*) and/or synergizing their abilities (*what they could not*), whereby the total effect is greater than the sum total of the individual abilities. Leaders are the catalysts, the individuals who get the process going. *Leader* is a noun and *leading* is the verb. Whether you agree with this definition or not, it explains how I'll be using it.

To make this whole thing even more confusing is that people who are managers are often called leaders, yet managing is quite different from leading. So the goal of this chapter is to help you understand what those differences are, as well as figure out which situations require managing and which ones need leading. Although this book has "manager" in the title, the fact that most managers oversee groups of people working together to accomplish goals leads us to assume that managers should be able to lead when it is required.

Based on these definitions, we can then determine what is and is not leadership and leading, and therefore who isn't a leader (assuming an authentic leader leads). So just being the boss and in charge of others doesn't necessarily make you a leader. Whether your title says "manager" or not doesn't mean you're a leader.

The typical manager must lead *and* manage. Managing has to do with focusing on a project, a set of tasks designed to accomplish a goal. The typical manager is also in charge of a team of people who work together to accomplish these tasks. The human side of the process is typically leadership. Thus, you can combine the two to determine how you'll develop your self-image as a leader and get things done. The person who fails to combine these two aspects will usually be ineffective as a manager.

Most managers fail in the area of their people stills, related to leadership-oriented qualities, because they've usually been promoted based on elevated technical skills and/or seniority. The focus of this book is on helping you understand how to avoid the most common weakness of managers: developing their team members to accomplish projects together. It's simple to say, "Managers must help teams be effective," but getting to what this really means takes a whole new way of thinking.

The Leading-Managing Compass

Another way of looking at your role as a boss is to think about it like a compass. A compass is an instrument (before GPS) that helps us find where to go, based on four main points, north, south, east and west. On any given day, or even sometimes multiple times in a day, you'll need to pull out your compass and determine what kind of boss you need to be in terms of what your organization needs. The compass will also help you recognize differences between leading and managing. Leading (north) tends to focus more on people and less on tasks. That doesn't mean that leading isn't concerned about the tasks, but rather the emphasis is on the people, whether that means motivation, development, or organization. Conversely, managing (south) is more task-focused. As opposed to leading, managing means that tasks are on the front burner of the stove and people are on the back burner. On the right (east), the goal is to innovate, to make changes. On the left (west), the goal is to do what is necessary to keep things going as they are-- maintaining the systems, processes, and outputs.

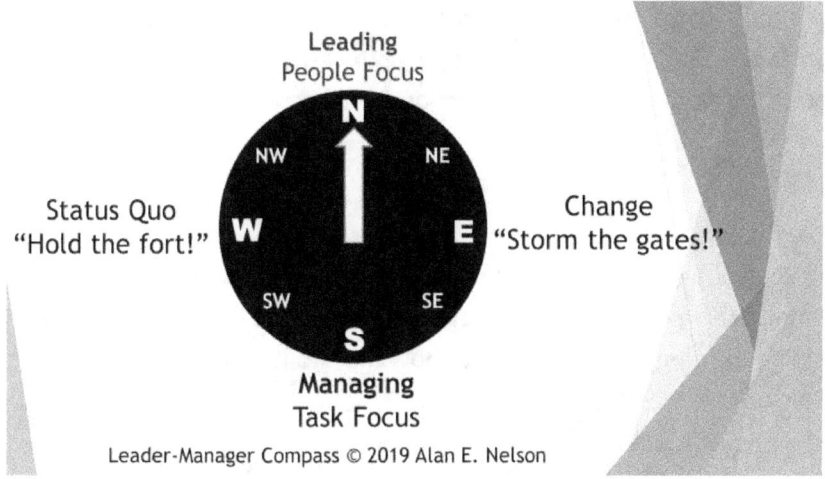

Leader-Manager Compass © 2019 Alan E. Nelson

So what do the corner directions involve?

NE is when a leader must help people move in a new direction. This might involve vision casting, motivation, and more relational skills that are needed to get people to embrace a new idea and implement change. Usually this is proactive.

SE is more about the implementation of new ideas, involving some of the nitty-gritty details, whether it's implementing a new software program, assigning new tasks to various teams, or providing resources to make needed adjustments.

NW is when a leader must respond to forces that seek to destabilize the organization. This may involve encouraging people to stay the course, or perhaps recruiting new talent to keep things going.

NE involves managing systems that create stability and thwart changes that might damage the organization. The focus here is on getting the right processes in place and implemented, so that things run smoothly and responsibly.

This is what bosses do—figure out what direction is needed at any given time. As you can see, if you're heading to the southwest when you should be going northeast, you're going to end up in the wrong place. If you're only familiar with one direction, you'll be a lousy navigator.

Comparing Leading and Managing

Now that we've defined leadership, leaders, and leading, let's compare this to qualities of managing. Look at the two lists below. Both focus on accomplishing organizational goals, aligning people with resources, and helping the company succeed, but how they do it and how they are wired are different.

Leading	Managing
Vision & strategy	Policies & procedures
Creating value	Counting value
Change oriented	Complexity oriented
Aligning followers	Organizing subordinates
Macro/big picture focused	Micro/detail focused
Appeal to the heart/emotions	Appeal to the head/logic
Sets directions	Plans detail
Asks strategic questions	Gives tactical answers

People-task balanced	Task-oriented
Influence & inspiration	Power & control
Proactive	Reactive
Less risk averse	More risk averse
"Storm the gates"	"Hold the fort"
Does the right thing	Does things right
Where we're headed	Day-to-day operations

I'm not going to unpack each concept, but if you think of each circle of characteristics as a collage of paint strokes on a canvas, you begin to see the differences between leading and managing, regardless of the title you give to the person doing them. Some books make you think that managing is poor leading, but it's not. Poor managing is ineffective managing and good managing is effective managing. Poor leading is ineffective leading and good leading is effective leading. They're complementary but different processes. So while the title of this book, "Five-Star Bosses," is a bit of a misnomer, we use the word because most people who oversee a team or division of people are referred to as bosses. But don't be misled!

Naturally, you'll need to adjust to the terminology of your organization to avoid misunderstandings, but you may want to do some educating on these ideas with your team members so there's better clarity and expectations.

When to Lead

I grew up on a farm in Iowa. We raised cattle and hogs, alfalfa (hay) and corn. One day, my dad and I were standing beside our neighbor's soybean field. About 50 feet from us, sticking out from all the low bean plants, was a 4-foot tall corn stalk. My dad pointed to it and asked, "Do you know what that is?"

I looked at him, puzzled, because we both knew what it was since we had acres of it on our farm.

I said, "That's a corn stalk."

My dad said, "No, it's a weed."

"That's no weed," I argued. "It's corn."

Then he explained, "Any plant that's not supposed to be there is a weed."

The same is true when it comes to organizational behavior. Managing when leading is needed makes it a weed. Leading when managing is needed turns it into a weed. Even though I'm a huge advocate of effective leading and have invested much of my life studying, writing about, and teaching leadership, I'll be the first to admit that leadership isn't always needed. In fact, when everything's going well and an organization is really humming, then avoid leaders at all costs, because they'll try to change things. Leaders are proactive thinkers, always pondering what else could be done. That's not always appropriate.

Conversely, most of the time you need effective managing, because someone needs to take care of the current business or else we're all sunk. That's why in start-up organizations, entrepreneurs who are unable to develop systems and people who maintain them will eventually fail. History is full of stories of new ventures that take off, only to crash and burn because the visionary leaders could not manage things well and were unwilling or unable to implement a support system.

So what are the qualities of a situation that calls for leading versus managing? Here are five symptoms to know when to wear the leader cap.

1. *When significant change is needed.* Leaders are all about change. That's why you want to avoid them when everything is flowing smoothly. This type of change has to do with pursuing a new goal or opportunity. It's the process of getting everyone on board to adopt something other than status quo. The idea of change requires people to get out of their comfort zones in order to think differently and accept new ideas. The ability to create space to pursue change while taking care of business as usual is in and of itself a unique skill set.

2. *When you need to touch the hearts of your team members.* Managers tend to work from a more cerebral, cognitive approach to convincing others, but leaders emphasize the heart, creating a felt need to follow you. This emphasis may involve a change, embracing a new team member or process, or simply motivating people to put in extra effort to make a deadline. The impetus on people and relationships is key here. You're not just managing a project, you're rallying the troops to storm into battle, small or large. Leaders get people to follow them.

3. *When you need to tap the power of others.* Leaders deal with power. Power is latent ability to move others. Influence is power-activated. This power may come from people who report to you, colleagues who are equal to you, or those above you who possess authority resources to make things happen. The ability to persuade others to accept your ideas and plans is truly a leadership quality. Recognizing who needs to offer buy-in and how to convince them are specific skills that effective leaders possess.

4. *When a new system is being introduced to your team.* This is obviously related to change, in that it refers to an external issue that you're forced to adopt. This may come from a supervisor, the CEO, or even a significant external stakeholder who wants something different. Managers tend to react to these with more negative attitudes. But leaders make lemonade out of lemons. You rally the team to embrace the challenge and face the issues, whether they be budget cuts, role transitions, or embracing members from a new merger or acquisition. Leaders know how to win over the hearts of people, creating the extra energy required to adopt a new system imposed by an entity with more power.

5. *When people need to be motivated, inspired, and unified.* Synergy is when the product of the group exceeds the sum of the individuals. Leaders synergize their team members. When your team members are bored, experiencing conflict with each other, or simply need to be motivated, leadership is required to unite them. A manager tends to rely on authority, threats, and even coercion to get others to do their jobs. But leaders take the high road, inspiring them to overlook pettiness and pursue a higher objective. This can be done in a number of ways, depending on the resources, situation, and chemistry of the team. The bottom line is that leaders make this happen. Managers do not.

Grappling with the differences between leading and managing is not easy. Yet, effective managers understand that differences exist. Knowing what these are and when each skill set is required empowers them to get the job done effectively. When you are in a position where you need to both manage and lead, your ability to change hats at a moment's notice is supreme. Reading the situation allows you to be appropriate, so that others are amazed at your ability to lead and manage. This is a difficult opportunity that provides ways for you to leave your mark and impress others with your expertise.

Five-Star Boss Questions:

1. List two or three aha's you got from this chapter.
2. What other situational factors would you add to this list of when leading is needed?
3. What questions did this chapter raise for you?
4. Why do you think so many people use leading and managing interchangeably?
5. Based on these qualities, would you describe your supervisor as more of a leader or manager?

Chapter 5

The Supervision Continuum

All Influence Is Not Created Equal

When you're the boss, people look at your differently. They have assumptions and expectations of what you should do, whether or not they ever tell you. This is referred to as implicit leadership, the image we perceive of an effective person who is in charge. That's why so many people can love any given President of the United States while at the same time, many others loathe him. While you won't make everyone happy, a Five-Star Boss does an excellent job of providing what the situation requires. Part of that is understanding how you're wired along with what type of supervision is needed. Five-Star Bosses are wired for what is required.

Let's look at a model I've developed called the Supervision Continuum. This is a graph representation that depicts how all boss influence isn't the same. Just because a person is a supervisor (boss) doesn't mean that person is a leader. So, for the sake of communication in this chapter, we'll refer to supervision and boss as the same thing. Every person who is a supervisor or a part of management has some kind of influence, but that doesn't make that person a leader. Leadership covers a specific span and type of influence. As we go through a brief description of each of these types of influence, think of people in your organization and consider how you're wired. Then decide where you'd place yourself on the Supervision Continuum.

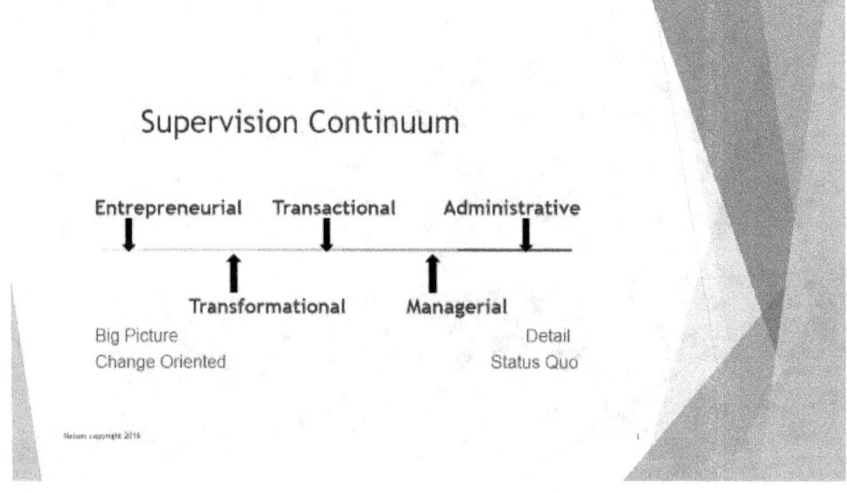

Entrepreneurial: On the left side of this graphic, you'll find entrepreneurs. Some are truly leaders; others are inventors only. A person who comes up with a new way of doing things isn't necessarily a leader. The entrepreneur starts new things, but those who lack strong leadership abilities are usually either replaced by someone else or they experience the crash and burn of a potentially great organization that never created the systems required to perpetuate it. This is common among start-ups, where the visionary launches strongly but doesn't implement processes to manage growth and create stability. Sometimes, very brilliant entrepreneurs can create sufficient momentum where others follow.

Transformational: This is a type of leader who understands how to cast vision, move people emotionally, and get others to follow a dream and vision. The transformational leader is vital for new organizations and turn-arounds, because they're designed to catalyze large scale improvements in organizations. They touch us in the heart, use inspiration, and activate emotions. The stereotypical transformational leader is charismatic and dynamic and ignites the passions in people. A limitation of this person is that often s/he isn't able to see the details and tangible path for making the dream a reality. Studies show that transformational leadership is more influenced by genetics than its counterpart, transactional leadership, thus it's more difficult to learn.

Transactional: This supervisor is still a leader, but not transformational. The transactional leader focuses more on the head than the heart, possessing an ability to make incremental changes by logic, exchanging rewards for services, and helping others feel confident in a plan. The role of the transactional leader is to help the organization progress in steps versus leaps and bounds. Although this style isn't as "sexy" as transformational leading, it tends to be more stable and strategic. When large changes employing people are needed, a transformational leader will often trump this person, but otherwise, effective leaders like this are just as (or more) successful over the long haul. They're also more common, as transactional leading is more easily developed than transformational leading.

Managerial: To the right of the transactional leader is the manager, who leans toward maintenance, status quo, and more detailed work. We discussed the difference between managing and leading in the previous chapter, so consider those qualities here. Some people speak negatively about managing, referring to it as bad leadership. Conversely, these people suggest that good managing is leadership. Actually, bad leadership is bad leadership and good management is good management. They're different skill categories on the Supervision Continuum. Effective managers keep things going, deal with problems strategically, help teams function well, and are comfortable overseeing day-to-day operations.

Administrative: On the right side of the Supervision Continuum is the Administrator. This person is focused on dotting the i's and crossing the t's. An effective administrator is strong at holding people accountable and making sure things get done on time and efficiently. S/he troubleshoots the systems. These people are important because they keep the company out of legal problems and management members from going to jail. Administrators can wield a lot of power, but their strengths are not typically seeing the big picture, taking risks, or catalyzing change. They counterbalance those on the left side of the continuum by mitigating the risk of their weaknesses, just as those on the left bring strengths that administrators lack. This accounting, engineering, and introspective mindset allows them to think deeply about details as well as keep the ship afloat. Most administrators do not lead, but they can certainly influence people and organizations.

Implementing the Continuum

A model is often a convenient fiction, striving to organize and simplify complex situations. Yet, as someone said, "There's nothing as practical as a good theory." The Supervision Continuum is a tool to understand why individuals with influence aren't good at everything and why each role can both thwart and catalyze progress. Five-Star Bosses are good at surrounding themselves with people who make up for their weaknesses. The human temptation is to surround ourselves with clones, because we relate to them and think the way they think. But this will eventually damage the organization.

There's nothing wrong with being any one of these people, but pretending to be someone you are not will create intense stress and cause a lot of pain to the organization. A positive way of saying it is that there are not wrong people, just wrong situations. A more honest approach is to acknowledge that administrators will create severe damage if put in charge when transformation is needed. But when things are going well, an organization is better off with a manager, someone who's strong in systems thinking and operations. Obviously, medium to large organizations usually need a key executive in each of these influence styles.

The Supervision Continuum is a simple way to communicate that all influence isn't the same and that while each of these roles possesses power, power can be as destructive as it is constructive. It's also a helpful way to offer labels that honor each role as opposed to conveying the idea that if you're not a leader or even a certain type of leader, then you're less of a supervisor. The bottom line is that names and titles can be confusing, whereas identifying types of influence and identifying those most able to use them assists us in understanding who is needed in specific situations as well as why some may not be as effective as we hope. No one person can do it all, so matching needs with abilities is vital for organizational health.

Five-Star Boss Questions:

1. Where would you say you are on the Supervision Continuum?
2. Where do you think other people with influence in your organization are located?
3. Do their roles seem to fit how they're wired? If you had a magic wand, how would you improve things?
4. How was this helpful? What questions does this create?
5. What do people expect from their bosses?

Chapter 6

The Two Key Boss Qualities

The DNA of Leadership Trust

The Power Pair

Studies show there are two things employees want most from their boss, and they're essential if you want to be an effective boss. The two qualities are competence and compassion. Those interested in following you want to know if you're capable of leading, helping the team achieve, and understanding your business. Plus, they want to know if you care for them as people, have their backs, and value them as team members. These two ingredients build trust, which is the currency of leadership. Without trust, you're toast. At the most you'll get compliance, but not commitment. (We'll deal with these two concepts later, in another chapter.) The first element creates *competence trust,* and the latter creates *caring trust*. We don't follow people we don't trust. Both are essential.

You've probably known people who were caring but incompetent. They didn't make good decisions and they were, well, not very smart. Don't confuse education with smarts. I've taught for over 20 years, but I've met some very educated people with few smarts. I've also met some really intelligent people who barely made it through high school. Common sense isn't that common.

So when you're the boss, you need to think about both of those qualities. If you're overly task-oriented, people will think you don't care about them and they'll hold back. And if they like you because you're fun to be around and value them but they don't trust your ability to make decisions or understand what is going on, then they'll also hold back.

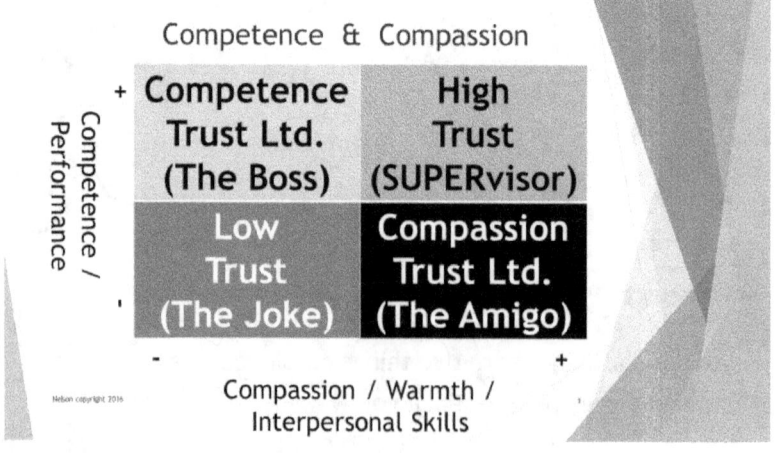

High Competence / Low Compassion (**The Boss**): The upper left quadrant represents a number of new managers who get promoted because of their technical skills. They're good at sales, engineering, accounting, or marketing, so as more senior employees exit, they're the natural insiders for promotion. Yet managing projects is quite different from managing people. I call this person The Boss, because s/he is under the impression that if you want people to do something, you simply boss them around. These are the tellers, the supervisors who seem to flaunt their authority and as a result, get people to follow them not because they want to but because it's required if they want to keep their job. They find it difficult to get things done because trust is limited to competence.

Low Competence / Low Compassion (**The Joke**): The lower left quadrant is typically occupied by the person who isn't respected because s/he lacks know-how and people skills. This manager may have gotten the position because of who s/he knows (i.e. the owner's son or CEO's niece) or was merely in the right place at the right time and no one else had seniority. Sometimes it's because upper management is desperate or preoccupied with more important problems when the need for a new manager arises. Sadly, Jokes are usually ridiculed behind their backs. People make rude comments, roll their eyes, and if they don't quit or transfer, exhibit passive aggressive behavior that decreases team performance and outcomes. Jokes find it very difficult to get things done because trust is so low.

Low Competence / High Compassion (**The Amigo**): The lower right quadrant is occupied by managers who are appreciated for their positive demeanor but not respected as competent leaders. The Amigo (friend) is more of a congenial colleague who is in over his/her head. The role of the Amigo is one of support, appreciation, and empathy, but at the end of the work week, team performance suffers because the manager lacks the know-how required for understanding how things get accomplished. The Amigo can't bring out the best in others because s/he doesn't know what "best" is. People typically prefer working for the Amigo versus the Joke or the Boss, but the fulfillment that comes from performing at a high level is rarely achieved. Amigos are liked but not respected. When pressure comes from above or a crisis happens, the Amigo becomes the butt of jokes and comments because s/he doesn't have the bandwidth to know what needs to occur. Amigos have a challenge getting things done because trust is limited to caring.

High Competence / High Compassion (**The SUPERvisor**): The upper right quadrant is obviously the place to be, if you're able, because here lie men and women who understand their job from both a technical and people aspect. SUPERvisors may not be the most experienced in technical skills, but they know who to rely on and bring out the best in people. A SUPERvisor needs to know enough about the business to recognize who to engage and how to recognize good work. They often aren't the smartest people on the team. Henry Ford said that he hired people who were smarter than him. Know-how thresholds vary, depending on the industry. For example, I'm aware of a school district in the Los Angeles area that hired a superintendent who'd never been a classroom teacher or a principal, yet he came from Los Angeles Unified School District (LAUSD) as a proven leader. LAUSD is the 2nd largest school district in the United States, so he understood educational administration and is proving to be a smart choice. But just down the road, at Jet Propulsion Laboratory (La Canada Flintridge), a manager without a modicum of scientific experience wouldn't be taken seriously. The point is that a person with both technical know-how and people smarts is typically an exceptional manager. SUPERvisors typically see great results from their leading because trust is high.

Developing Trust

Although this is a focus on issues regarding competent trust and caring trust, let's take a quick peek at trust in general. The etymology of the word *trust* includes "help, confidence, protection, and support." Because trust is the DNA of effective leading, managers who lack trust, because they made a bad decision or offended team members, need to know how to grow it. Think of trust like a plant in your garden that requires water, fertilizer, and good soil. Five-Star Bosses are good gardeners. That means they know how to water, fertilize, and provide adequate nutrients for their "plants" to thrive.

Three critical ingredients to regain trust are humility, time, and substance.

Humility: If the boss pretends he didn't make a mistake when others know it, others trust him less. Humbly acknowledging the offense, owning up to the decision made, and making apologies as needed are all vital factors for trust to grow back. It's akin to the gardener hoeing the soil so it can receive the seed and water. Bosses driven by ego, too proud to admit a failure, create a toxic working relationship. Team members will invest unnecessary time discussing the fault and striving to catch him in future failings.

Time: Trust is like good wine, cheese, and meat, requiring time to season. There's no such thing as instant trust. The closest thing is called "calculus trust"—the trust we offer strangers based on goodwill we see in most people. But when a boss loses this, there is a time factor required for people to forgive and gradually risk following you again. Although we can forgive people instantly, trust doesn't immediately grow back. Savvy leaders understand that and avoid taking advantage of others' forgiveness.

Substance: Time alone doesn't grow back trust, in that people need to regain a sense of why they can and should trust you. We can set up situations to create trust, such as empowering team members to make decisions. The context determines what this looks like. But the more people see that you're both competent and compassionate, the more likely they'll eventually let go of the past and begin trusting you more. Obviously, the greater the mistrust, the longer it takes to grow it back. Consistency is important, so they see over time and in a variety of situations that you are indeed worth being followed. Someone said that after being burned by a hot stove, a cat won't sit on a hot stove again. Of course, it won't sit on a cold stove, either.

Five-Star Bosses balance the two most important factors people look for in their leaders: competence with the task and care for the team.

Five-Star Boss Questions:

1. Think of an example of a leader who overdrew his/her trust account. Was it primarily about competence, compassion, or both?
2. Why do you think people value both competence and caring? In your experience, which do bosses lack most?
3. Describe a time someone betrayed your trust. How did it or could it grow back?
4. Why do you think trust is so important for managing/leading?
5. What could you do to improve your team members' perception of your competence?

Chapter 7
Uber Thinking

The DNA of Effective Decision-Making

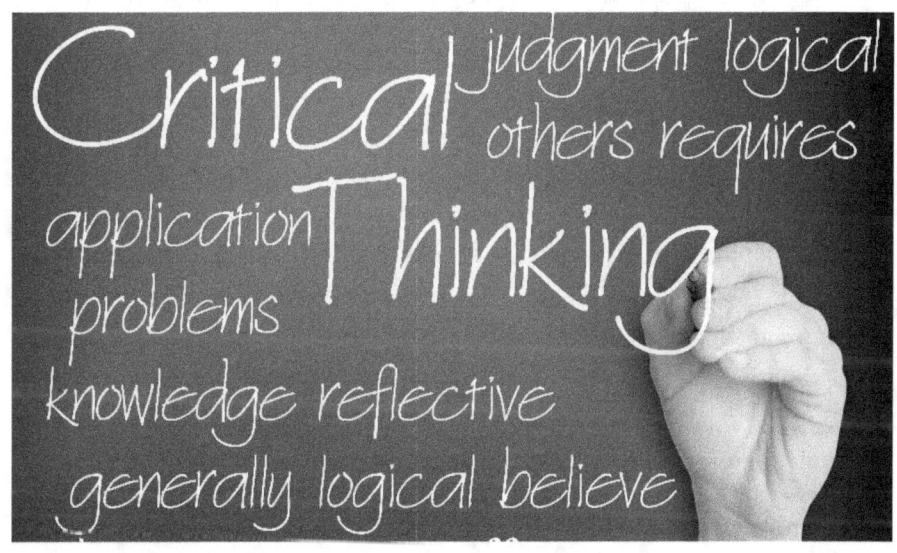

The 4-D Solution

A young manager attended a luncheon where the speaker was a renowned bank president. After the event, the manager waited in line to talk to the senior leader.

"How did you get to be so successful?" he asked the banker.

"By making good decisions," the speaker responded.

"How did you make good decisions?"

"Wisdom."

"How did you get wisdom?" the young manager asked.

"By making bad decisions," the banker answered.

There is certainly truth in the older leader's response. Your success as a boss will rest heavily on your decision-making ability. So, while we learn a lot from our failures, a way to avoid needless bad decisions is by applying critical thinking. The word *uber* refers to an outstanding or supreme example of a particular kind of person or thing. This chapter is a quick overview of the process that you can use alone or with a work team. Each of the four steps begins with a "D" to help you remember the process.

Diagnosing the Root Problem

Critical thinking begins in correctly understanding the main problem. When a physician diagnoses, she looks at the symptoms but wants to discover what caused them. If you only address the symptoms, you aren't getting to the root of the problem. One problem in an organization can produce a lot of "fruit," so you want to uncover the root. Although you may need to respond to multiple issues, you want to avoid merely putting a bandage on a broken leg.

A simple way to do this is to make a list of problems. Then, like a family tree, create a visual that clarifies which ones are symptoms (offspring) of the problem "ancestor." For example, if revenue is down, a plausible solution is to increase marketing. But if the root problem is the entrance of a better technology by a competitor, you'll likely be wasting money in marketing an antiquated product and thus not find the solution you're seeking. Lively discussions emerge as people share their perspectives, but this is often necessary to properly identify a root problem. What is the cause of the situation (root) and how can we avoid being distracted by symptoms (fruit)? The reason you need to clearly identify what you believe is most apt to be the root problem is that your solution should match it. Thus, an error at the start will result in a faulty outcome. Most seasoned leaders agree that more time should be invested in studying the problem, as less effective bosses tend to be quick to propose a solution to fruit versus root problems.

Determining Alternatives

Once you think you've identified the main problem you want to address, you'll want to come up with 2-4 plausible solutions that address this. Make sure they focus on the problem you want to abate, not the array of issues identified, unless you have a specific reason to do otherwise. You may come up with more than this number, but finalizing a list of 2-4 forces you to prioritize the ones most beneficial. Each alternative describes a potential solution. Describe each in 1-5 sentences. Then state 2-4 strengths (pros) of why this is good. Then list 2-4 risks (cons) and/or potential weaknesses of the alternative.

Being honest about the pros and cons is important, because rarely will you have a potential solution without a downside. When people ignore what they don't want to hear, they increase the size of their blind spot, setting themselves up for disappointment and failure. You may want to formally designate one of your team members as the "Devil's Advocate," whose responsibility it is to verbalize weaknesses. This helps prevent someone fearing being perceived as negative or anti-team oriented when suggesting potential dangers in the plan. "Hey, I'm just doing my job as the 'Devil's Advocate.'"

Deciding on a Solution

After listing the 2-4 alternatives, you'll want to select the one you believe will yield the highest ROI (return on investment). Although it's tempting to combine the benefits of two or three of the alternatives, you should avoid this by coming up with a distinct hybrid alternative in the previous step. The hybrid will have its own set of pros and cons. The reason for this is similar to why a physician needs to understand the medications a patient is taking before prescribing a new one, because sometimes meds have adverse reactions to each other. When you combine characteristics of an alternative (potential solution), you may inadvertently be mixing pros and cons that interfere with each other.

Remember, the solution should be related directly to the root problem (versus a fruit problem). If it does not, then you need to go back and verify what the root problem is and how it's different from the symptoms and side issues. If for some reason you need to address one of these, based on an issue of urgency or to buy you extra time, then make that explanation when you clarify the problem. Upon deciding which alternative is the best one, you should include the following aspects:

1. *Include implementation details and examples*: As the saying goes, "The devil is in the details." By offering some specifics in terms of how you'd activate the solution, you can avoid impractical conceptual solutions that will never be implemented. These don't have to be detailed, but should provide examples of what you'd do. You may include task assignments, ways to measure the progress, and offer timelines.

2. *Mitigate the risks*: The word *mitigate* means to soften, make mild or gentle. When you listed the potential solution in the alternative section, it should have included some cons (risks). These don't go away now that you've selected it as the best idea in the batch. In fact, they may actually grow because now you're activating them. So, what can you do to lessen the negative impact of the solution? How will you increase the odds it will work and that the pros (benefits) will be realized? This is an important part of improving your ROI.

Deploying and Improving
Obviously, critical thinking has to be grounded in reality. That means that even the best minds can't determine on paper what will fully work after implementation. The cycle is that you diagnose the problem, determine alternatives, decide on a solution, and then deploy it. When

you deploy, you'll see opportunities to improve, change, and mitigate further for the purpose of improving the outcomes. Although pilots submit flight plans, determining where they intend to land, much of their trips they're making adjustments based on wind vectors, payload, and other aircraft. Thus, at any given point along the path they are off course. The constant adjusting allows them to reach their desired destination.

Your work as a manager continues after the deployment of your decision because you'll need to re-evaluate and adjust. A report published by Harvard noted that typically, managers are only 60% informed in the decisions they have to make. A Top Gun fighter pilot friend of mine said it's the inverse in the military. They're making decisions with 40% or less of accurate intel. This is not due to laziness or lack of effort, but rather we can't fully predict the future. That's what we're striving to do in problem-solving for the most part—trying to lead our teams and organizations into the unknown. So, make sure that after you push the "Go" button on your decision, you review the outcomes and then implement the critical thinking model again and again.

Applied Critical Thinking

1. What are the primary issues (concerns, problems)?
    - What is the root (cause) and what are the fruit (symptom) issues?
    - What is the target issue (the one we need to resolve first)?
2. What are 2-4 ways to solve the target issue (alternatives)?
    - List the 2-4 top benefits (pros, pluses) of each
    - List the 2-4 top risks (cons, negatives) of each
3. Select the optimum alternative as the solution
    - How will you mitigate (lessen) the risks of it?
    - How will you implement it?

Implement the solution then re-apply steps 1-3

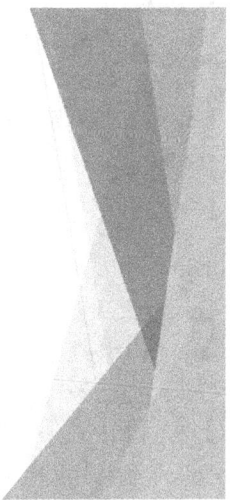

Critical vs. Cynical Thinking

Before wrapping up this chapter, I want to address an issue I've discovered, related to critical thinking. Some people confuse critical thinking with cynical thinking. These are not the same. In my work in higher education, I have the opportunity to interact with some very intelligent people, students with high IQs and great potential. Yet I see a common quality among many students; they're overly critical. These people confuse critical thinking with being negative, in that they tear apart ideas when they're embryonic and before they've had an opportunity to develop. For some reason, they think being smart and educated means ripping up ideas, focusing on the negative, and jumping to the dark side of suggestions. They do this with seemingly strong arguments and come across articulately, yet the end result is they're basically intellectual cynics. The last thing the world needs is an educated pessimist, telling us what won't work, why our ideas suck, and why they're so smart in verbalizing their critique. This is little more than a masquerade for cynicism and pessimism.

Leaders are purveyors of hope. Napoleon stated that several centuries ago. Five-Star Bosses are good at critical thinking, but they're also optimists. They believe that in spite of the way things seem, together we can create a brighter future, a more hopeful outcome. Therefore, if you want to rise to the top of your organization, you need to figure out how you can be both thoughtful *and* hopeful. A person lacking critical thinking skills will make mistakes that result in people losing faith about his/her decision-making prowess.

You can't afford to confuse critical thinking with being cynical, and you can't allow your team members to, either. You'll need to enlighten them on how the best thinkers come up with solutions that inspire people to believe, to do their best work and to improve the future. Your ability to catalyze hope in your team will make you a leader who others want to follow. Without this skill, you'll prove yourself to be a mediocre manager who does little to change status quo. Your team desires more from you. Even the people wired as pessimists want to believe that good things can transpire from their work. Don't let up. Don't allow the naysayers to prevail, regardless of their IQ and seniority. Do your best to convey hope, positivity, and optimism.

Five-Star Boss Questions:

1. Think of a situation where you observed an analysis of a problem and how it was resolved. Analyze it in the context of critical thinking.
2. How would you change it, to see better results?
3. Why do you think managers don't do better in terms of implementing the critical thinking model?
4. What impacted you from the paragraph about critical vs. cynical thinking?
5. What can you do to help others by being critical, not cynical?

Chapter 8

Decision-Making Blind Spots

Avoiding Perception Biases

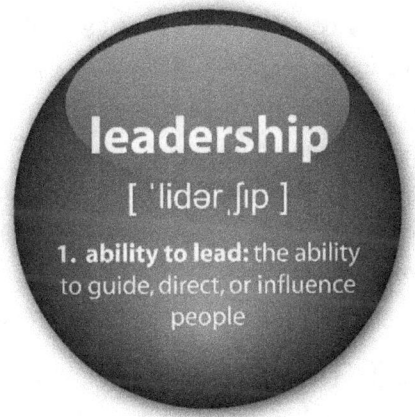

The Measure of a Boss

Although we can learn more from our failures than our successes, your effectiveness as a boss is directly proportional to your decision-making ability. Therefore, as much as possible, you want to avoid making bad decisions. This chapter's graphic uses the words "guide" and "direct" in the leader definition. If you can't see well, it's difficult to guide and direct people. But what impedes our sight and sense of direction? Faulty data cause planes to fly into the sides of mountains and people to drive the wrong way on the freeway. The same is true in making decisions. Let me introduce you to some of the most common perspective biases—issues that distort the way people see and think about information. I'll give you the skinny on 10 issues to consider during your planning, trouble-shooting, and crisis management meetings. Hey, I'll even throw in an 11th because I believe in you.

Availability (Satisficing): This bias bases decisions on information that is readily available but also quite limited. What often happens is you're sitting around a table during a meeting and someone asks something like, "What can we do to get the word out about this new product when our marketing budget is next to nothing?" This begins a mini-brainstorming session, based on the cumulative knowledge of the people in the meeting. A couple of people have dabbled in social media, another person has a friend who is a PR specialist, and another used guerrilla marketing tactics for a start-up he was a part of that incorporated handing out fliers and street corner signage. All of these may be viable ideas, but the sum total of the memorable experiences around the table limited the decisions made. Experts in the field were not contacted, no research was assigned, and yet, the success of your new product relied on the ideas available around the table.

Another type of this bias is referred to as Satisficing. Let's say that as the boss, you ask Kyle to do some research on the demographics in your area for people potentially interested in your new product. Kyle does a quick Google search and emails everyone the results. Everyone feels satisfied that the shallow search engine research was accomplished and that you performed your due diligence. This false confidence means you'll make a decision based on inadequate knowledge. It's the equivalent of a minor flashing a fake ID to get a drink without considering legal ramifications. Skimming the top appeases our burden of responsibility, creating a false sense of accomplishment.

Confirmation Bias: "Don't confuse me with the facts." You've probably heard that cliché. When we make a decision, whether formally or simply in our mind, our brain searches for information that confirms it. For example, let's say you purchase a Honda Accord. You happened to do an internet search of recommended cars afterward, based on safety, reliability, and value retention. Your tendency will be to click on research and reviews supporting the superiority of Honda Accords among other cars. You'll shy away from information that suggests this make and model are troublesome and inferior. Confirmation Bias seeks information that substantiates a decision and avoids what is contrary to the decision made or desired. It happens when a colleague stops to discuss a problem for which he's already made a decision. You begin to realize that he's not so much interested in your opinion as he is seeking support for a conclusion he's already formed.

Escalation of Commitment: When you make a statement, you're putting a stake in the ground that is tied to your reputation and expertise. Naturally you want to defend it, because no one wants to look foolish or appear to be naïve. But most statements are based on opinions, meaning they're not 100% sure. Even if we're 80%, 90%, or even 95% confident that we're right, the tendency is that the more we argue in support of our claim, the higher our confidence grows. Nothing in the evidence has changed. The bias lies in what we initially thought as opposed to how we feel after we dig in our heels and drive the stake further into the ground. Many times I've had a debate with my wife about some trivial matter, but in the process of defending my position, I end up in an exaggerated over-statement of the case. My goal was more about winning the debate than verifying the facts.

This bias is also referred to as Sunk Costs. Projects we've already invested in will tempt us to invest more, to avoid losing what we've already put into the project. The phrase "throwing good money after bad" refers to this perspective issue. Let's say you've invested $25,000 in a new software program that's not producing the results you wished. Instead of cutting your losses and purchasing another program, you decide to spend $10,000 more in upgrades and training. While this may not be a bad idea, the tendency to invest more instead of changing gears was influenced by an Escalation of Commitment bias.

Halo Effect: This perception bias is most commonly seen in celebrity endorsements. It has to do with transferring a person's qualifications in one area to everything the person does. For example, LeBron James promotes Beat headphones by Dr. Dre'. Although LeBron is a noted expert in basketball, we know nothing about his ability to analyze audio technology. Regardless, his endorsement elevates the public's confidence in the brand because of the Halo Effect. You see this come into play when another company (i.e. Google, Apple) behaves a certain way and then someone in your organization suggests you should adopt the practice. Just because an expert in another arena suggests an idea doesn't mean you should embrace it, or else you could become a victim of the Halo Effect.

Attribution Theory: Nearly everyone has succumbed to this bias. The concept is that we tend to attribute good qualities to ourselves and negative ones to others. It's self-serving in nature. For example, when we succeed at a task, we base it on the fact that we're smart, hard-working, and ethical. When someone else succeeds, we tend to attribute it to politics, cheating, or dumb luck. We also, unconsciously, look at how a person behaves in other situations, how society (small or large) behaves, and how consistent the person is in this area. For example, let's say that Frank is late to work one morning. If he's nearly always punctual and if the office culture is that everyone begins at 8 a.m. sharp, then we'd think that Frank must be stuck in traffic, sick, or had an accident. It's an external cause. Conversely, if Frank is frequently late and/or the office policy is flex, then we'd attribute his tardiness to how Frank operates. It's an internal cause.

Overconfidence Bias: The proverb states, "Pride goes before a fall." The error of this bias is when people make decisions based on past success and/or a basic overconfidence in their skills and knowledge. One of the reasons that 20-somethings experience this perspective bias more than others is that their lack of experience limits their wisdom in terms of what can go wrong. Thus, they tend to overestimate their ability and take inordinate risks by overextending their resources and underestimating expenditures and time. One way to circumvent this bias is to refer to veteran colleagues and/or hire consultants. The goal is not to avoid risk-taking but to mitigate inordinate risks.

Primacy Recency Bias: The idea behind this perspective weakness is that we're significantly influenced by first and last experiences. "You only have one opportunity to make a good first impression" is a cliché referring to primacy. Research shows that the two most impactful events, thus elevating the chances these will be recalled in a person's memory, are the first and last impressions. For example, if you're doing a speech or sales presentation, it's better to go first or be last, because your receivers are most apt to remember and thus offer you a better response (so long as it's done well). When you ask people about their favorite eateries, chances are they'll share positive examples from more recent experiences, even though they've eaten at 100s and 1000s of restaurants. When reality TV shows present an array of contestants who dance, sing, or perform other talents, they'll nearly always begin and end with their strongest because they want to hook you into watching and leave you with a positive memory. So how does this affect you as the boss? Be wary of over-relying on stories, suggestions, and examples from first and more recent experiences, because you may be overlooking more noteworthy examples stuck in the middle. If you're interviewing several candidates in a row, be sure not to overlook strengths of those in the middle. Our memory plays tricks on us that can impact decisions.

Anchoring: This bias pertains to the influence that an initial statement or number has on subsequent ones. The brain tends to compare and contrast opinions based on the first statement, the "anchor." For example, let's say that you spin a roulette-type wheel and it stops at 85. Then you ask a group of people whether they think the percentage of new businesses in the last five years that are women-owned is higher or lower than this number, most would say "lower." When you ask them to offer an estimate, they say "40%." Now let's say you spin the wheel again for a different group and the number is 19; asked the same question, most would say "higher." But when you ask them to offer an estimate, they say "30%." So while the Primacy bias says that first impressions are lasting ones, Anchoring bias implies that initial facts or statements influence our views about subsequent ones. The difference in saying 40% and 30% had nothing to do with facts but rather a random number that influenced our comparison.

Stereotyping: Most of us are familiar with stereotyping, the human tendency to lump people into categories and then label them based on very little evidence. Yet most people don't consider the evolution of this natural inclination. Back in cave-people days, when we heard a noise and saw a bush move, we needed to decide very quickly whether the animal behind the shrub was going to be our lunch or if we were going to be its lunch. This initiated the fight or flight mechanism in the brain, a survival technique that required us to respond quickly. The practice of stereotyping therefore has healthy roots, when our brains have limited time and resources to identify and determine if another is an ally or enemy. Guess wrong, and you could be in big trouble. The weakness of the practice is when we use it too often and with few checks and balances. We compare a few traits of one person, such as gender, skin tone, facial features, or language with a person or people we've interacted with who possess similar characteristics. We then identify them with other qualities based on culture, traditions, hearsay, and others' opinions. If and when you hear someone on your team say things such as "Men are..." or "Women aren't..." or "Asians always..." or "Millennials don't..." then chances are decisions are being based on distorted perspectives. While rooted in primal instincts, it can invade modern decision-making without us realizing it.

Groupthink: There are numerous aspects of this, but the overarching idea is that people behave differently in groups than they do alone. Sometimes the chemistry of a small number of individuals working or socializing together create an atmosphere where decision-making is adversely affected by the social chemistry. Here are some of the distortions that reflect Groupthink.

- Overconfidence and risk-taking: Groups often feel less immune to failure and tend to take greater risks than individuals.
- Rationalization: Groups tend to justify their decisions among themselves and think of themselves as more moral than others.
- Stereotyping: Groups can have a tendency to demonize those outside the group.
- False unanimity: Because peer pressure often silences naysayers, a lack of speaking out can be labeled as agreement.
- Pressure to conform: When one or two individuals disagree with the others, they can be intimidated to remain silent and to go with the group. This is the root of the NASA Space Shuttle Challenger disaster, when engineers were silenced about raising concerns regarding the adverse effect that a low launch temperature might play on the O-rings. The launch resulted in a catastrophic explosion, killing all seven aboard.

Framing: Imagine that your team is on the third floor of an office building. Each person is in front of a different window, looking out. One person describes seeing a park. Another disagrees, seeing a parking lot. Someone else convinces the rest there are trees outside the window. This is a simple illustration of framing, describing what you're seeing through your lenses. It's why police try to separate witnesses of a crime or accident, so each doesn't influence the other. Framing is being influenced to believe what another person says based on the way he or she says it. That's why when negotiating, it's more productive to frame the situation through your eyes than it is to convince others that what they're seeing is wrong. Politicians are notorious for framing the same set of data from significantly different views. Persuasive people are adept at framing, convincing others what they say is correct, whether or not it is.

Decision-Making Biases

Availability (Satisficing): info limited to a small search
Confirmation Bias: selecting info that supports our opinions
Escalation of Commitment: failure to cut losses due to investing
Halo Effect: transferring one quality to everything a person does
Attribution Theory: assuming the best of us, the worst of others
Overconfidence Bias: thinking we're better than we are
Anchoring: influence a first fact/statement has on subsequent ideas
Primacy Recency Bias: first and last impressions are strongest
Stereotyping: categorizing entire groups on a few perspectives
Groupthink: effects of groups on skewing reality
Framing Bias: the influence on how things are presented

People do not respond to reality; they respond to their *perception* of reality. So while critical thinking is an important process in decision-making, Five-Star Bosses realize we're all prone to perspective biases that impact the way we process information. It explains why smart people can look at the same set of circumstances and come up with significantly different solutions. Your ability to recognize and defuse common biases will empower you and your team to make higher performance decisions, resulting in a reputation for leading well.

Five-Star Boss Questions:

1. Which of these 11 perspective biases have you seen at work in your organization?
2. Think of a recent poor decision you or your team made and do an autopsy on it (AKA post-mortem). Which of these perspective biases may have influenced the decision?
3. Which of these do you think you're more susceptible to committing? Why?
4. How can you plan in advance to mitigate this risk?
5. How can you introduce these biases to your team in order to make your meetings less susceptible to them? (Idea: consider making laminated cards or a poster of these for team members to have in front of them during meetings.)

Chapter 9
The C-Word
The Boss's Kryptonite

Transition vs. Change

When I was a kid, one of my favorite TV shows was Superman. My mom would safety pin my blanket around my neck, creating a cape. I'd fly from the couch to the ottoman, mimicking the Man of Steel. The only weakness of this superhero was kryptonite, an element from Superman's planet of origin. Other than a limited aptitude for leading/managing, the boss's kryptonite is a six-letter word: *change*.

Next to leadership, change is my favorite topic to study. That's probably because change is the main thing leaders do. They transform people's aspirations, challenge status quo, and help their organizations move ahead. How you as a boss respond to change will make or break you as a supervisor. You will experience two aspects of this issue. One is how you catalyze change in your team or division. The other is how you respond to changes required by those above you. The goal of this chapter is to give you a fast overview of the key aspects that can undermine your effectiveness or make you an invaluable asset to your company. Someone said, "Change is inevitable, but growth is intentional." The fastest way to die these days is to keep things the way they've been. Between the speed of technology, the pressure of global competition, and the social changes created by media, the kiss of death is to keep doing what you've always done. We used to think change-oriented orgs were limited to high-tech companies, but the paradigm has changed. Today, the only constant *is* change.

Chances are as a boss, you won't be responsible for creating large-scale innovation in your organization, but you will be asked to implement changes required by upper management. And you'll likely be able to initiate changes related to your team, division, and area of responsibility. Therefore, it's important to understand the basics of change and how people respond to new ideas and processes so you can assist your supervisors in improving the likelihood their ideas will be implemented. Few upper management people have studied the change process.

In his classic book *Managing Transitions*, William Bridges describes the difference between change and transition. A change has to do with a physical, external difference, such as new software, an outside competitor, or a corporate takeover. Transition has to do with the inner, psychological shift that must take place to accept the new thing. He states that transitions take us down far more than the changes themselves. Another thing Bridges points out is that leaders tend to sell the solutions. That's a mistake; they need to sell the problems. People aren't shopping for a solution for which they do not perceive a problem. Thus, if you want your team or division to embrace a new idea, make sure you put more time into establishing the need for it. Someone said, "You can lead a horse to water, but you can't make it drink. Although you can feed it salt." So how do we create a thirst for our ideas before we propose them?

Two Plans

If you want to implement significant change in your organization, you need to plan. But one plan won't suffice; you'll need two, an Improvement Plan and a Transition Plan. The first is more traditional in terms of stating what you're going to do and what you want to achieve. It includes resources, people, money, and timelines. But a Transitions Plan is not about the *what*; it's about the *how*, referring to the process of selling the idea to decision makers and then those who'll implement it. As you can see in the list of qualities (figure below), they're quite different.

Improvement Vs. Transition

What we plan to do	How we plan to do it
▸ *Where are we going?*	▸ *Where are we at now?*
▸ *Resources/structure*	▸ *People/culture*
▸ *Mind/logic*	▸ *Heart/feelings*
▸ *Left brained*	▸ *Right brained*
▸ *Know how/talent*	▸ *Relationships/influence*
▸ *Risk/boldness*	▸ *Patience/perseverance*
▸ *Managerial/strategic*	▸ *Leadership/vision*

Let me comment on a couple of the listed items that may seem counterintuitive. A Transition Plan looks at *where we are now*, because merely looking at where you want to go is incomplete. For example, one company may want to make $10M in sales, but they're currently at $8M. Another company plans to hit $10M, but they're only at $5M. The difference between where you are and where you want to be will impact how you make the transition. The greater the distance, the more stressful the process will be.

Another factor is *patience/perseverance*. This means you'll need to counterbalance risk/boldness with empathy, because your people will need to be heard and not yelled at. So while both plans exhibit unique qualities, they are complimentary and need to be accomplished in tandem.

Psychology of Change

As Bridges noted, emotional adjustment to change is the main reason people push back on new ideas. Therefore, it's easy to understand that personalities respond to changes differently. One author who used the Myers-Briggs Type Indicator as a filter suggested that over 70% of people are averse to change. They prefer sameness. In his classic book *Diffusion of Innovations*, Everett Rogers categorizes people in terms of how they respond to new ideas. I've tweaked the names to make them more neutral.

Creators: Only 2-3% of people are Creators, those who come up with new and often out-of-the-box ideas. They sometimes are perceived as flighty and a bit odd by the majority, but they love ideas simply for their newness. The value they bring is initiating risks and innovations. Their challenge is being accepted by the large majority and having little patience with slower adopters.

Progressives: This group comprises 10-15% of a company, depending on the type of organization. A Progressive is open to workable new ideas, and they're strategically situated to influence others. They're generally positive about change, so you'll want to include them on a transition team. The value they bring is an openness to new ideas and influence with the next group. Their challenge is boredom with status quo and a lack of patience with slower adopters.

Builders: Another name for these people is the early majority, consisting of 34-40% of a given org. They're generally open to a new idea that seems logical, but can sometimes get stuck in the details and will reject ideas that aren't obvious to them. They're unwilling to be the first ones to try something but will follow the lead of others, so long as they see good results. Their value is in helping faster adopters think about the value of new ideas. Their challenge is getting stumped by the details and coming across negatively.

Foundationals: This group is also known as the late majority, consisting of 34-40%. The challenge of these members is that they're highly unlikely to embrace a new idea or process until they see a number of Builders embracing and valuing the innovation. The value of Foundationals is they make faster adopters see potential problems overlooked. The challenge is that they can come across as negative and keep the organizations they serve from taking advantage of windows of opportunity.

Anchors: This is the tail end of the adoption groups, equivalent in size to the Creators/Progressives (12-18%). These people tend to be very reticent to adopt a new idea or innovation and will usually only embrace it when forced to do so. The value they bring is helping us appreciate our heritage and learn from history. The challenge is creating a negative influence within an organization that needs to make changes. Their negativity is often a mask for fear.

Urgent: Read This!

One of my favorite authors on the subject of change is John Kotter, a former Harvard professor. Kotter notes eight steps that effective change processes go through. We won't unpack them here, except for one. Kotter noticed that about 70% of change efforts fail, primarily due to a key issue: a perceived lack of urgency. Establishing a sense of urgency is a primary responsibility of leaders. It separates the change issue from other important matters. We all know we should eat right and exercise, but then your doctor says, "If you don't change your nutrition and activity level, you'll be dead in six months." Now it becomes urgent. So how can you make the innovation an urgent matter? If you do not, your people will eventually put it on the shelf with other things. But false urgency is akin to crying "wolf" when there is none, so building a case of why time is of the essence is key for leaders striving to catalyze change.

The Four Factors

Over the years, I've read a plethora of books and articles on org change. As a result of this research, I've developed a 4-factor model called the Nelson Change Formula (NCM). It's a practical tool for discussion related to how effectively the change will go. Although I can't reduce the entire model into a single chapter, I will give you an executive brief on each of the four factors and how they interact with each other.

Leader Umph: How much leadership ability does the person in charge possess? Because leaders are change agents, the stronger the leader, the better the chances for the transition to happen. On a 1 to 5 scale, 1 being low and 5 very strong, what is the leader's "umph"?

Influencer Readiness: A second factor is who the other Opinion Leaders are. Whose "yes" or "no" will make a difference on whether or not the idea is accepted? List each person, along with a score of 1 to 5, 1 being they'll fight it versus 5 they'll fight for it. Add the total and then divide by the number of Opinion Leaders to come up with an average score. This does two things: helping you identify who has an opinion that matters and estimating where each stands regarding the innovation. A good change agent will likely need to meet individually with each Opinion Leader and specifically know what s/he likes/dislikes, so their needs can be addressed.

Time: A third factor is how fast you plan to implement the new idea. Most leaders make the mistake of pulling a time goal out of the air, with little consideration for how important time is to a change effort. As a boss, this may not be flexible for you if it's mandated by upper management. But know that the less time you have, the more stressful the change will be. People need time to adjust to new ideas and emotionally prepare for their implementation. Extending time usually lessens stress. On a 1 to 5 scale (1. 1-6 months, 2. 7-11 months, 3. 1-2 years, 4. 3 years, 5. 4-5 years), what's the time factor?

Idea Impact: The fourth factor estimates the difference the idea will make on the organization. A small idea won't make a big impact, but a large innovation can change a company's DNA. Let's use an analogy of heart care, to illustrate a 1 to 5 scale. A 1 would be equivalent to a doctor suggesting a change in diet and exercise. A 2 is the equivalent of prescribing medications. A 3 on the scale would be angioplasty. A 4 would be by-pass surgery, and a 5 would be the equivalent of a heart transplant. Make sure not to over- or under-estimate the impact an idea will make on the life of your team, division, or organization.

Transition Index Results

Transition Index: As you can see from the simple, mathematical formula (next figure), after you plug in the numerical estimates for the four factors, you come up with an index. This estimates how effective the transition will be. Granted, it's an estimate, but it offers a communication tool to raise issues that often get overlooked. The model also provides a process for analyzing various issues that hamstring change efforts. Although a lousy idea won't turn into a great one with an effective transition plan, the reality is many wonderful ideas fail because they're implemented ineffectively.

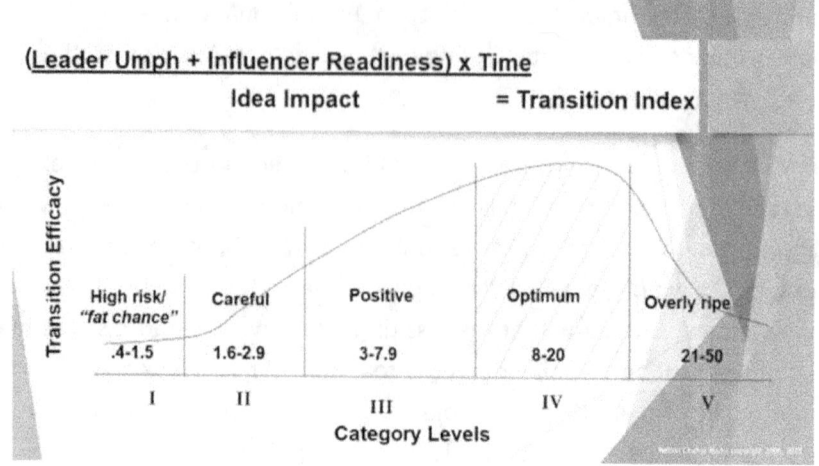

The above graph identifies five categories predicting what you can expect if you move forward with the change in the current situation. Following is a brief explanation of each one.

Category I: This is a *High-Risk* scenario. You'd better make sure the change is worth the risk, because it's going to cost the organization a lot. The patient may not make it off the operating table. People will quit. Leaders may get fired. You may lose your job if you're perceived to be a part of the change agency. The worst result of change in this category is that in the future, people will be prone to avoid innovations because of the pain created by similar innovations.

Category II. In the *Careful* category, the patient may survive, but there will be significant presence of pain. If the idea is the right one, it will benefit the organization over the long term. If not, people will become jaded and the leader will lose credibility as a result of transitioning so poorly. Avoid pushing a new idea in this category because it will cost a lot, even if implemented. It will take time to recover from the transition before advocating even more changes.

Category III. While *Positive* may seem good because the idea will be adopted, you can expect some ruffled feathers, hurt feelings, and reticent adopters. Assuming the idea is an effective one, people will come to embrace it and eventually appreciate it, but for a while there will be a tentativeness. Perhaps the biggest danger of this category is the temptation that you don't have to do anything. This attitude will result in unnecessary pain and costs that could be avoided with better preparation.

Category IV. The *Optimum* category is the most desirable, yet an effective boss will still want to prepare the team, communicate well, and help people as they process the new idea. The overall reaction will be positive, but some of your later adopters will feel nervous and be resistant. Even in *Optimum* situations, people will feel the stress of making the change. Yet, if the idea is a good one, people will feel empowered and know that over the long haul, they'll be better off than before. As much as possible, strive to create a Transition Plan that results in your organization being in this category.

The most strategic ways to adjust a non-optimum plan is to adjust the Time and increase Opinion Leader (OL) Readiness. Investigate why you need the time selected and see how you can add to it. The latter strategy is accomplished by understanding what each OL objects to in the innovation and then address these issues, either through education, emphasizing benefits, and/or addressing the perceived fears. The next option may be to reduce the size of the change and/or decrease the number of changes, thus reducing the Idea Impact size. The least likely strategy is to increase the Leadership Umph. The alternative to this is to wait until a new leader takes over, in case the leader is retiring or another rotates in, as in the military.

Category V: While some may suggest waiting until everyone is onboard with a change, when you do this, you'll have lost opportunities for potential gains. Plus you'll have frustrated your progressive people who desire results. The *Overly Ripe* category lets fruit rot on the vine and thus is not a viable solution, but rather a result of abdicating leadership.

Hopefully you can use some of the ideas shared to help avoid unnecessary pain during change processes. Your ability to catalyze and navigate these in your organization will make you an invaluable asset. Effective change agents are rare, so your stock will go up as you assist upper management in accomplishing their needed adjustments.

Five-Star Boss Questions:

1. Think of a change initiative you've experienced in the past. Do a postmortem on it, based on the content in this chapter. That means go back and analyze what went well and didn't so you can learn from it.
2. What's a current or upcoming innovation that's facing your organization? How can you apply this info to better understand it?
3. Who are the Opinion Leaders in your organization? How are they wired?
4. What is a change you think would make your team/division/company more effective? Run it through the Nelson Change Model.
5. What would be an effective Transition Plan?

Chapter 10

SWOTting Your Org

Analyzing Strengths, Weaknesses, Opportunities & Threats

SWOT* Power

Thinking strategically is a leadership skill. You're responsible for your organization's effectiveness. One popular strategic tool is a SWOT analysis. If you're familiar with a SWOT, naturally you can skip this chapter, but if you're not, you'll discover a helpful technique for analyzing your organization as a whole (or at least the portion you oversee). SWOT is an acronym for strength, weakness, opportunity, and threat. Self-awareness is to an individual what a SWOT is to an organization. It's great to do a formal SWOT analysis with your team when you're trying to figure out a new change, market, service, or product, or when a competitor is moving in on your area. A SWOT can be highly involved, but its power comes in offering a quick summary of the internal/current and external/future positives and negatives.

Some suggest that the phrase "SWOT analysis" is actually inaccurate; it's more of a summary of an analysis. Therefore, you'll want to be able to explain the rationale behind the ideas you put in your SWOT. Although you can do a quick SWOT on the back of a napkin in a coffee shop, it's usually more effective if a team develops it because the perceptions and discussions are helpful to gaining a more strategic insight into your team/division/company's health and future.

A SWOT is based on two axes. One identifies whether the characteristics are internal or external. The other labels them as positive or negative. Another way of looking at it is strengths and weaknesses are present tense (now) and opportunities and threats are potentially in the future—what could occur. The following graphic shows a 2x2 matrix that displays the information.

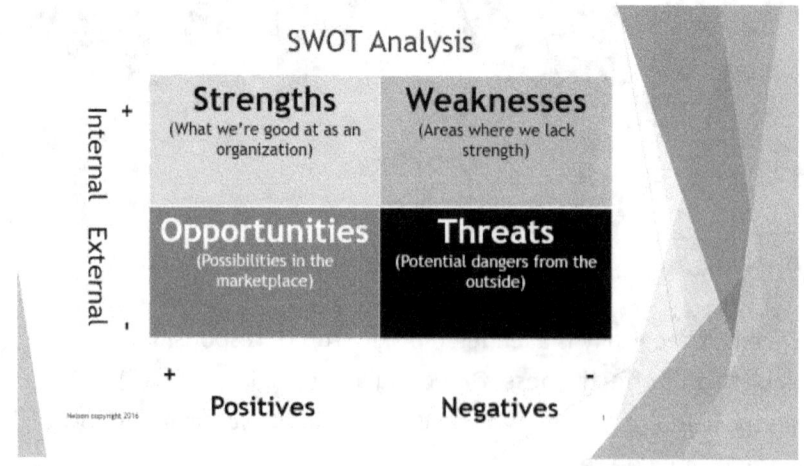

Strengths: What does your organization do well, now? What are its most positive attributes? When compared to other similar organizations, what would be its more favorable characteristics? These are items to include on the strengths list. They are important for you to consider, because when you're around them a lot, sometimes you take them for granted. Characteristics may be processes, values, staff, training, leadership, recruitment, heritage, product excellence, or any number of other attributes. If you have a long list, consider the top strengths. Typically, you'd shorten the list to 3-6 items. You can do this for a team, department, division, or entire company.

Weaknesses: The inverse of strengths is weaknesses. These are internal, pertaining to your organization, not things outside of it. What are its faults, now? What creates problems due to internal issues, such as staffing, budgeting, management, and processes? Is your marketing or sales department weak? Do you see the need for training, leadership succession, or strategic planning? Is there employee turnover? Are people in tune with the vision and direction? If you could change 3-4 things about your organization, what would they be? These questions help identify weaknesses if they aren't readily obvious to you. Again, you can do this for a team, department, division, or entire company.

Opportunities: An opportunity is something in the environment that will benefit your organization or that you want to pursue. It's what you might become in the future. Again, this is not about "opportunities" to reduce weaknesses; that's internal. Naturally, your strengths may match up with taking advantage of certain ripe conditions in the marketplace or environment. It's what you can pursue and/or become in the future. What is a growing market you want to seize or a technology that will give you a bigger advantage in your industry? What is emerging that might benefit what you do?

Threats: What's a potential danger up ahead? What are the wolves howling near your home? Who are your competitors? What are their strengths? How do they align with your weaknesses? What would happen if the market fell from beneath your company? How might these align with your weaknesses? Distinguish what is internal (now) from what is external (tomorrow). What is in your blind spot, perhaps a threat that you don't see or don't take seriously? If the organization was not around in 10 years, why would this be?

These are examples of things to look at and how to categorize them.

Short bullet-points or even a word or two for the main features of each item are sufficient for the graphic and can be explained otherwise. The other benefit of writing the summary points and putting them together is that it creates a stronger awareness of how these items may interact with each other. How are the threats and weaknesses in line or, conversely, how might the strengths combat the threats? How might strengths play into seizing opportunities, or how could they be missed due to internal weaknesses?

As you work on a SWOT, you'll also gain a better awareness of how others see your organization. This alone can be educational, understanding how they think and how accurate you perceive their views to be. The conversations can create healthy debate and even some effective conflict. The SWOT is also a way to communicate with colleagues, subordinates, and superiors as a quick tool for conveying your analysis of your company.

Example

Following is an example of a SWOT graphic for a popular and widely known company, Starbucks. I include an array of SWOT bullet points pertinent to when I wrote this chapter. But organizations and environments are always changing, so you may want to review the items and consider which of these you'd edit based on what is going on in Starbucks and the marketplace now.

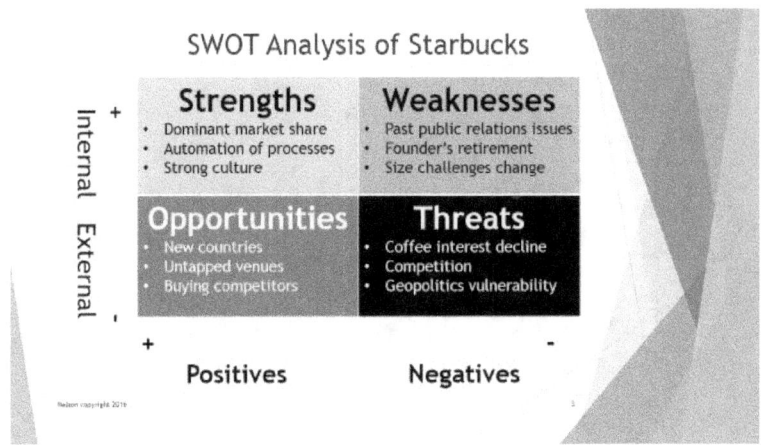

Five-Star Boss Questions:

1. On a sheet of paper, draw one vertical line intersected by one horizontal line. Label each quadrant at the top and bottom of the paper, like the SWOT graphic in this chapter. Then for your organization, list at least three strengths and three weaknesses and at least two opportunities and two threats.
2. Discuss these with a colleague or your team members.
3. What are the strategic benefits of doing this annually and when changes are looming?
4. What are the potential risks of not doing a periodic SWOT?

*The SWOT was created by Albert Humphrey in the 1960s at Stanford University. He was studying data from many large companies, to learn more about what goes wrong in planning. His original model actually was SOFT (Strength, Opportunity, Fault, Threat). Someone later changed Fault to Weaknesses and it became popularized as SWOT.

Chapter 11
Social Banking

The Power of Bartering Influence

Influence Currency

When I travel to China, I use Renminbi to purchase things. In Thailand it was the Baht, in Europe the Euro, in Dubai the Dirham, and in Peru the Nuevo Sol. Knowing the currency of the culture is essential to getting what you want. I'm not trying to get all academic on you right now, but there are a couple of popular theories related to leadership and motivation that can help you when it comes to influencing people to get what you want. Obviously, bosses need to influence those below, beside, and above themselves. One leadership theory is called LMX, or leader-member exchange. Leaders get things from those they lead, and followers get things they're looking for from their leaders. For example, I'll follow you as a good boss, because I'm apt to get a paycheck, fulfillment, and opportunities to grow in my career. Leaders gain talent, time, and work effort from their team members, toward the accomplishment of goals that are important to their careers as a boss.

Another motivational theory related to this is called Expectancy Theory. This is the idea that people are motivated if they get what they expect from a reasonable amount of investment, so long as they're able to perform at a sufficient level. Plus, they must like the outcome and reward, meaning it has value to them. People are demotivated when they get less than is expected or if they don't value what they receive. Expectancy Theory helps us understand why people work harder for things they value achieving and less when they don't think they're likely to achieve and enjoy them.

The Bank

Now imagine that each of your team members has an account in a social bank you own, where they make deposits and withdrawals (like at a financial institution). Not only do all of them have accounts in your bank, but you have an account in each of their banks as their boss. Your name is on your account, and you also make deposits and withdrawals, carrying a daily balance that goes up and down.

These social bank accounts are affected by how much people value what we do for each other. For example, if one of your team members arrives early, stays late, and has a positive attitude, s/he is adding to her/his account in your bank. You value that person and appreciate what s/he brings to the team. As a result, when this person wants a specific day off or extra resources, such as a bigger office or flex schedule or longer lunches, you're more apt to comply. The person's request is a withdrawal, reducing the social bank account balance available.

Conversely, when you do well as a leader, exuding vision and confidence and creating a positive work environment, you are increasing social units of currency in the accounts of others. They respect and like you. Because you carry a high balance, you're able to periodically ask them for special favors, such as working late or coming in on a weekend to meet a big deadline. These withdrawals lower your balance, but as long as you are aware of it, maintaining a positive balance will keep your team members engaged and committed.

The inverse is true as well. When your direct reports disappoint you, arrive late and leave early, and display a negative attitude, they'll be "underwater" when it comes to benefitting from what you can give them. And when you underperform as a boss, demanding more, expressing a critical attitude, and never seeming satisfied, you'll carry a deficit in your ability to ask more from them. Your employees won't value you as a boss, which will decrease your influence.

One problem in social banking is that a deposit and withdrawal are in the eyes of the beholder. If you think you're positive and respectful but your team members feel like you're curt and demeaning, you'll assume you're adding credits when in fact your balance is decreasing. It's akin to the positive and negative exchange rates you experience when you're traveling internationally. Sometimes your money goes further than at home, and at other times it buys less.

Influence

Unleash your influence not authority. -Joseph Wong

One of the best ways to influence people is to make them feel important. -Roy T. Bennett

Your influence on others is your networth, treat it as such. -Peprah Boasiako

Having influence is not about elevating self, but about lifting others. -Sheri Dew

Influence: What you think you have until you try to use it. - Joan Walsh Anglund

The people who influence you are the people who believe in you. - Henry Drummond

You can't influence people you refuse to associate with. -Andy Stanley

So the only way on earth to influence the other fellow is to talk about what he wants and show him how to get it. -Dale Carnegie

Your circle of influence dictates your path. -Jon Bielecki

Effective Accounting Practices

Hopefully you get the analogy, so assuming you do, here are three principles you'll want to consider when you're social banking as a boss.

1. **Know your balance.** Balancing your checkbook means knowing at any given time how much money you have in the bank. The same is true with social banking. At any given time, you should have a pretty good estimate of how many social credits you have in your account in their minds, as well as what they have in yours. If you have a big ask coming down the road, a project that's going to require all-hands-on-deck or extra work, you'd better make sure you accrue positive inputs prior. Conversely, if you've been a bit edgy, critical, or overly demanding, you may not have sufficient credits to ask for more. If you make demands, people will pull back, behave passive aggressively, or even quit. Social banking is dynamic, so today's balance isn't necessarily the same as next week's.

2. **Understand your rate of exchange.** What are the things your team members value? Some like public recognition, others time off from work, and still more appreciate bonuses. What can you do to customize your rewards to what your members appreciate? Avoid a constant leak of social credits by being bossy, grumpy, negative, and overly demanding. No one enjoys a boss who is pessimistic and surly. Conversely, have you communicated what constitutes a deposit in your account? Do you prefer face-to-face communication or emails? Do you like more or less feedback on a regular basis? Do you value employees who are punctual, tidy, well-dressed, or not?

3. **Make strategic withdrawals.** The goal of social banking is not to build up as much as you can and live off the interest. When you do this, the organization suffers. The aim is not your popularity, but rather the value you bring to your company. Periodically, when you have a high balance, you need to make a significant withdrawal, whether it's an organizational change process,

pushing to accomplish a big goal, or asking team members to give more during a downturn in the economy or covering shifts and tasks of others. If you're afraid of making withdrawals or if you make them for frivolous and non-productive asks, you won't be an effective boss.

The goal of this system is to act proactively. The bottom line is that social banking is going on, whether you understand it or not. The reason people go through divorces, experience staff splits, and see lackluster results from team members can be explained through the lens of social banking. Knowing how much you can withdraw and making sure your deposits outweigh your withdrawals is important. Bosses who are oblivious to these three principles will run into problems and feel frustrated as to why they don't get more out of their team members.

Office Politics

Before finishing up this chapter, I'd like to offer insights into office politics. Even if you have no offices, you're going to have politics. The word derives from a Greek word referring to *people*. Every person's body maintains a temperature, typically around 98.6°F. Raise it a mere 3°, and that person has a notable fever. In the same vein, every group creates politics. It's the natural result of humans intertwining. But when an infection is present, the org becomes feverish and unhealthy. So when bosses say "We'll have no office politics," what they mean is they want people to get along with each other and be healthy in their relationships. A lot of that has to do with Social Banking. Knowing that you can never avoid politics in office settings is important to embrace. People will talk about you because you're the boss and possess power. Their opinions will include positive, neutral, and negative tones. That's what people do, so don't let this make you paranoid or insecure. Another word for an insecure boss is an ineffective boss.

Your job is to help people play well together, much like a parent does among siblings and a teacher in a classroom. Those who never learned how to share, clean up their messes, or take turns will create a fever in the workplace. Your role is to educate and coach your team. This helps them be healthy. If people aren't getting along on your team, it's your job to figure it out. So while you'll never be able to eradicate office politics, you certainly don't need to fear it or be held hostage by it. We'll talk more about this in the Managing Conflict chapter.

Five-Star Boss Questions:

1. Think of an example of a leader who overdrew his social credits and as a result, couldn't get what s/he wanted from her/his team members. Describe this situation.
2. List examples of what your team members would consider deposits. What can you do to increase your balance?
3. List examples of what your team members would consider withdrawals.
4. What are some current or upcoming situations where you can invest your social balance, asking your team members to give extra?
5. Describe an office politics situation through the lens of the Social Banking metaphor. Explain who offended whom; who had a stronger relationship with whom; and how could things have gone differently with better "banking" principles?

Chapter 12

The Big Five

Identifying Great Team Members

What Makes a Team Great

As I've mentioned, I'm honored to teach at the University of Southern California (USC) Marshall School of Business, in the Management of Organizations (MOR) division. But in addition to academics, USC is known for its athletic teams. One of the buildings on campus is dedicated to honoring the Olympic and professional athletes who played there. The university has had more Major League Baseball recruits than any other NCAA program*, and the perennial football powerhouse attracts some of the finest talent in the sport, many who go on to play in the NFL. That's in addition to NCAA championships in volleyball, water polo, and other sports.

Identifying and recruiting great talent is important to developing a great team. But the ability to work well on a team often supersedes individual talent. A group of *prima donnas* who can't work well with others or get along with the coach/manager will nearly always get beaten by lesser talents who understand the power of synergy. This is when $2 + 2 = 5$, meaning the outcome of the group is greater than the sum total of the individuals. Research shows that exemplary team members are rated high in five qualities. So while you can't ignore the importance of recruiting for the right kind of talent based on your needs, just as important is finding those with a strong ability to serve well on a team. Five-Star Bosses recognize that team skills transcend IQ and technical skills, because it takes only one person to mess up an entire team.

So let's look at a classic model proven to be an effective way for identifying great team members. It's called The Big Five, because it includes five qualities known to be exhibited by great team players. Four of the five also relate to Five-Star Bosses, so as we describe them, we'll see if you can guess which one doesn't fit them.

Think CANOE (or OCEAN), or even rowing a canoe on the ocean, as this serves as a visual acrostic to remember the five qualities.

Conscientious: This refers to possessing a sense of responsibility, a burden of perceiving that others are depending on you and a desire to not let them down. A conscientious person has a sense of ownership in projects and on teams. This individual comes to work prepared, is willing to arrive early, stay late, and do what it takes to get things done.

Agreeable: An agreeable person avoids dominating a conversation, is open to hearing the opinions of others, and if s/he supports a minority view, is willing to go with what the team decides. The latter is done without a passive aggressive attitude. Agreeable people make it easier to be on a team and are more pleasant to work around.

Neurotic: I'm not sure why the originators of The Big Five used the term neurotic, because it's obviously a liability. The inverse is a strength. In other words, the higher your neuroticism, the less effective you'll be on a team. A more positive way to describe this quality is stability, a person who responds well to pressure and remains optimistic when stressed. This also relates to emotional and social intelligences (read the chapter on Emotional Intelligence), the ability to understand and manage your emotions as well as those of others.

Openness: This quality is about being open to new ideas. Is the person curious and willing to try a new restaurant and/or order something new on the menu? This quality is vital when you need the team to adopt a new practice as a manager and when peers share varying ideas. An unwillingness to adopt new ideas and practices is a team killer. Sometimes you can discover this during interviews by asking the person to describe an example of embracing a new change, or asking the person how s/he would respond to going to a new restaurant and letting someone else pick the menu item.

Extroversion: An extrovert in this context is someone who possesses strong social skills and is comfortable sharing ideas, asking questions of others, and divulging personal issues. Even a person who is wired as an introvert, meaning s/he gets energy from being alone, can convey strong social skills when needed. The ability to be gregarious in social settings is vital to relationship building. A person who is quiet, avoids contact with team members, and stays to himself/herself would not be rated high in this trait. Most organizations cater toward extroverts, even though introverts can offer high-quality ideas, talents, and skills. Obviously, having team members who speak up and socialize well tends to benefit the quality of a team.

Using The Big Five

Think of colleagues/team members: Rate 1, 2, 3 for each of the five factors, using the following key:
1 Low, 2 Medium, 3 High (Total & Discuss)

- **Conscientiousness:** reliable, responsible, efficient, organized vs. easily distracted, unreliable, easy-going, careless
- **Agreeableness:** friendly, compassionate, cooperative vs. cold, challenging, detached
- **Emotional stability:** positive under stress, secure, confident vs. anxious, insecure, sensitive, nervous
- **Openness to experience:** inventive, curious, creative vs. consistent, cautious, conventional, comfort w/ familiar
- **Extroversion:** social ease, energetic, outgoing, gregarious vs. timid, reserved, solitary

The Missing Quality

At the start of this chapter, I challenged you to consider which of the five qualities Five-Star Bosses tend to be lower on than productive team members. The correct answer is Agreeableness. The reason is that leaders must be willing to go against the views of others at times. If you're unwilling or unable to do this for fear of what others will think of you or because you desire harmony on the team, you'll sabotage yourself. Leaders need to be able to make tough calls. They need to say "no" when others say "yes." So while you want to convey an agreeable attitude, Agreeableness becomes a weakness when you're in a supervisory role

So while the Big Five is a very practical model, it's not as helpful when you inherit a team. You can teach it to your team, but that's probably insufficient to change the way people are wired. The Big Five can empower you to recruit the right people to your team. Talk to any veteran manager and s/he will tell you that it's far easier to change a person's technical skills than it is their attitude. The Five-Star Boss puts far more effort into recruiting the right people than in trying to change people who are already on the team. The ROI is far lower when you need to improve one of these five qualities in a team member. So while talent is very important, the qualities that make for a strong team member enable that person to fit in and work well with others.

Five-Star Boss Questions:

1. Run the diagnostic on your team members that is highlighted in the graphic. Who scores high? Who scores low?
2. In your experience, where have you seen the weaknesses among team members?
3. What are subtle ways to uncover these aspects when interviewing a candidate?
4. Why is the quality of good teaming as or more important at times than technical skill?
5. How would you score yourself on these five qualities? How does your rating on Agreeableness help and hinder your leading?

*USC has produced 114 major leaguers over the years — more than any other NCAA program in the nation. Trojan alums boast 67 All-Star appearances, 29 World Series appearances, 9 Cy Young awards, 3 Hall of Famers, 3 Rookie of the Year Awards, 1 American League MVP and 1 World Series MVP (as of May 25, 2019).

Chapter 13
Motivational Strategies
The Art & Science of Moving People

Shhh, Keep This Between Us

The word *motivation* is from a Latin term meaning "to move." Getting your people to move is an essential skill of Five-Star Bosses. For the last few years I've taught MOR551 at USC Marshall School of Business, a course titled "Human Capital Performance and Motivation." Until I began teaching the class, I'd never significantly studied research and theories related to motivation, even though as a leader I'd served in roles where motivating people was essential. For many years I ran non-profit organizations where in addition to paid staff, I motivated scores of volunteers without the benefits of money, authority, or tangible incentives. So in this chapter, I need you to keep a secret. I'm going to summarize the entire course at USC in this and the next chapter. I don't want my students to find out about it because they'd likely rebel for the work I put them through. Let me give you a quick history of the theories so you can see the evolution. Then I'll introduce seven of them along with how you can use their wisdom in your work as a Five-Star Boss. The reason this is the longest chapter in the book is because, well, moving people is the most important thing you do, and Five-Star Bosses do this best.

The roots of motivation studies began in the realm of psychology. Freud suggested that motivation is primarily unconscious, the results of biology and sexual drive. After the turn of the 20th century, in the early 1900s, a man name Gilbreth did time and motion studies to help factories become more efficient. This was popularized by a man named Frederick Taylor. Taylorism, as it was called, focused on efficiency, along with incentivizing employees with money. Between 1925 and 1950, a guy named Rensis Likert came up with a way to measure employee satisfaction. Chances are you've taken a Likert survey, where you had to rate something on a 1 to 5 scale, with 1 being low and 5 being high. This tool measured people's opinions.

In the 1970s, behaviorism became popular, based on psychologist B.F. Skinner's theories of psychology. Skinner wasn't interested in the "black box," referring to the brain. He focused solely on actions, believing that employee behavior was a result of what they were conditioned to do—primarily, what they were rewarded to do. In essence, we get what we reward. This was a variation of Pavlov's experiments with animals, such as dogs conditioned to salivate after hearing a bell reminding them of food.

Abraham Maslow didn't like the way behaviorism was going, so he proposed a more human approach to understanding motives, widely recognized as Maslow's Hierarchy. He suggested that our basic need is physiological, as in food, water, shelter, and warmth. When these are fulfilled, we move to the next level: safety and security. After that comes love and belonging, such as family and friends. If these needs are met, we pursue self-esteem, the desire for recognition and respect. Ultimately, the top of the pyramid is self-actualization, the pursuit of inner fulfillment.

A 1955 formula by Maier stated Job Performance = Ability x Motivation. Someone later offered a formula for Ability: Aptitude + Training & Experiences. Then came theories focusing on expectancy, goals, self-efficacy, justice and fairness, and intrinsic motivation. These are a few of the dozens of theories that attempt to explain human motivation and performance. Following are seven of the more prominent theories, along with ideas for how you can use them in your work as a Five-Star Boss.

Time and Efficiency
The earliest performance and motivation studies focused on helping assembly line employees do better in factories (Taylorism). The focus involved making people more effective, such as timing how long it took a line worker to attach his parts to the moving auto chassis. Sometimes, raising or lowering a part, providing better tools, or moving a person closer to his work had the effect of improving behaviors. Money was seen as the primary motivator because employees were incentivized with performance levels. If Clyde could attach 10 bolts within five minutes, he'd receive a bonus in his paycheck at the end of the week. Poor performers earned less and could be removed from their positions.

While many manufacturing and assembly line jobs have left the U.S. and other Western nations, some of these concepts remain. The questions are "How can we provide the most effective tools and working environment for our people?" and "Is there a way of rewarding them for merit, based on performance that meets or surpasses our goals?" Naturally, this is highly contextual, but in places like call centers and in roles such as Costco cashiers, efficiency becomes a significant factor related to bonuses and promotions.

Theory X & Y
During the 1960s, an MIT professor named McGregor introduced a theory that pushed back on the idea that people needed to be prodded and yelled at on the job because they were inherently lazy and didn't want to work. That was a common attitude, but given the post-World War II boom of factories and mass production, assembly-line thinking

became a part of management. McGregor referred to this as Theory X. He proposed a different approach, Theory Y. Even though his original concept recognized some good qualities of Theory X, his emphasis is that instead of sticks, managers should focus on carrots. He believed that inside most people is a desire to achieve and succeed. Five-Star Bosses strive to figure out what the intrinsic motivators are (fulfillment, achievement, passion) as opposed to thinking only about extrinsic motivators (money, perks, power). While most of us are extrinsically motivated to a degree, we can gain exceptional performance when we tap into deeper motives. The challenge for you, as a Five-Star Boss, is to figure out what each of your direct reports seeks in a job. This empowers you to customize pay conditions and leverage issues related to deeper, stronger motivators.

Herzberg's Two-Factor Model

One of the big benefits to understanding employee motivation came when we began measuring satisfaction. Most managers think in terms of a single continuum, from highly satisfied to highly dissatisfied. But a psychologist named Frederick Herzberg introduced a two-factor model that places satisfaction and dissatisfaction on different continua. This model states that a person can experience both satisfaction with a job while at the same time feeling dissatisfaction created by other issues. For example, let's say you love what you do (high satisfaction), but at the same time you don't make much money (high dissatisfaction). Understanding both issues makes more sense, as it addresses the inner conflict we often feel in such a situation. By seeing satisfaction and dissatisfaction on different continua, you can improve the situation of workers. For example, you might date someone who has qualities you really like, but at the same time there are other issues that prevent you from wanting to marry the person.

Issues related to satisfaction have more to do with intrinsic issues, such as enjoying your work, finding purpose and fulfillment in what you do, and sensing that you're using your talents to benefit others. These are referred to as Motivators, characteristics that motivate us in our work and help us enjoy it more. These are often related to job design, organizational culture, and a sense of benefitting others or making a difference.

The other continuum is dissatisfaction, more extrinsically oriented. These are referred to as Hygiene factors, as they are related to the environment. They may include things such as pay, working conditions, flex time, childcare, training, and relationships. These qualities increase and decrease levels of dissatisfaction. High dissatisfaction can demotivate people who feel satisfied in what they do. They are also the easiest to address and therefore should be considered first when the goal is to retain good employees. But don't stop with Hygiene factors—also include Motivators that can increase satisfaction.

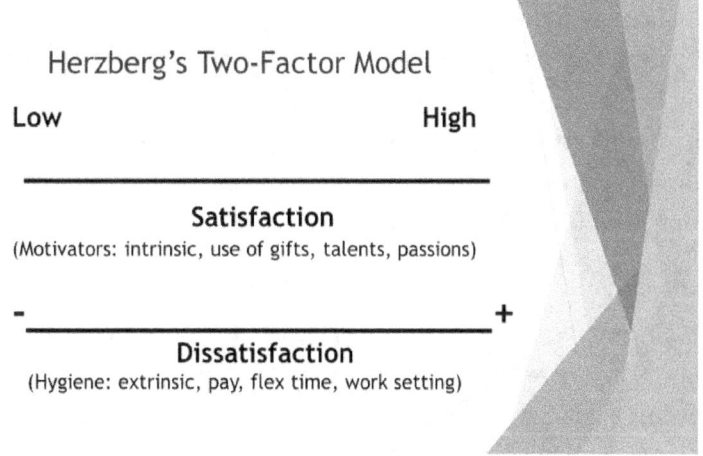

Don't Expect What You Don't Inspect

A former USC professor, Steve Kerr, wrote a classic Harvard Business Review article titled "On the Folly of Rewarding A, While Hoping for B" (1995). It's a great read. The gist of it is that most organizations tend to get what they're structured to get and most people do what they're rewarded to do. It's a bit Skinnerian, reverting back to Pavlov's conditioned canine; the first thing to investigate, if you're not seeing what you want and if you're seeing what you don't want, is the attention/reward system. By attention, I mean check out what gets measured and monitored. What do you ask for in reports? What shows up in job reviews? What is discussed in meetings? Savvy workers understand that everything listed in the job description doesn't get noticed, so the tendency is to stop doing what's not checked. The adage "don't expect what you don't inspect" applies here.

People tend to do what gets rewarded, both personally and systemically. Let me preface an example of this by acknowledging how much I enjoy being a part of the Naval Postgraduate School (NPS). It's truly an honor to be a Lecturer of Management there, serving the military and government employees. Some of the finest leaders I've ever met are in our military. Now that I've offered my accolades, I'm going to share a story that's common among government agencies and large corporations. The government is regularly seeking ways to cut costs, to make budgets stretch and do more with less. The problem is if you don't spend your allotted budget, you may not get it next year. That's why near the end of each fiscal year, huge and frivolous purchases are made in order to get rid of unspent monies and avoid losing next year's budget when it may be needed more.

One day I was visiting some course administrators at NPS. The three employees worked in an interior office without windows. When I walked in, I noted three large-screen TVs mounted on walls in a small space. One had a schedule of upcoming courses, another showed a webcam of the ocean from the nearby Monterey Aquarium, and the last had another outdoor scene. I said, "Wow, where did these come from?" The ladies grinned and said, "Someone from the tech department came in and said, 'You don't have any windows and we've got money left in our budget, so we're going to do something for you.' Sure enough, these showed up." A few weeks later, I was teaching a class on organizational behavior by video to a group on an East Coast naval base. I told this story and at the end, the students laughed, moving the webcam to three unopened large-screen TVs in the corner of their room. The point is that while management says they want to save money and cut costs, they actually reward spending 100% of the budget whether it's necessary or not.

No doubt you see behaviors and practices in your company that seem to conflict with stated goals and best practices. Most of the time, some sort of errant reward system is in place. Five-Star Bosses look for these in organizations, similar to investigating a leak in a low tire or the cause of a closet foul smell.

Expectancy Theory

A Yale business professor named Vroom introduced Expectancy Theory, a sort of model that analyzes a person's drive. The theory is based on three parts. I won't bore you with the academic version of the formula, but let me describe these components. The first has to do with analyzing the level of performance needed to get rewarded. People wonder, "What does it take to win the prize?" The second part focuses on personal ability, "Do I have what it takes to perform at this level, and how much effort will I need to expend?" The third targets the reward, "Do I value it?" This 3-step process is involved in most work environments, even if it's subliminal and not articulated.

A situation goes like this. Let's say John is on your sales team. He's told that during the 2nd quarter, if he improves his revenue by 30%, he'll receive a preferred parking slot, a 10% bonus, and dinner with the regional VP. John is thinking, *I'm barely making the quota now. It would take a lot to improve my sales by 30%, and my kid is in little league now and my wife's been harping about me spending too much time already at the office. Even if I improve 25%, I won't qualify for the rewards and to be honest, who cares about the parking slot and dinner with the VP. Forget the program, I'm sticking to what I've been doing.* John's expectancy is that the extra effort isn't worth it, so he's not giving anything more, in spite of management's intentions. He may smile, nod his head during the program info meeting, but at the end of the day, he's not taking the bait. The Expectancy Theory explains why John doesn't seem to be as driven as we'd hoped. While we may blame him or criticize his work ethic, in reality it's management's fault for not understanding what motivates people.

Job Fit

The power of this model is basically when managers have the opportunity to form-fit a job to the talents and passions of an employee. Although this has limitations based on the demands of the organization, the more you can do to shape a job to fit the strengths and interests of an employee, the more you'll get out of that person. This may involve things such as flexible scheduling, offering childcare, working from home, and creating merit-oriented rewards. Job Fit varies a lot from organization to organization, so you'll probably need to push the limits of your company's policies. For example, in my wife's profession of senior living care, employees can't work offline. They need to be where the clients are, in the facility. Punctuality is necessary so there's no lapse in care. Yet within those parameters, how you convey standards and hold people accountable goes far to set you apart from others. Five-Star Bosses advocate for their team members with their superiors and the larger organization. As a result, they gain respect and the commitment of their people. Naturally, you need to be realistic and understand that with freedom comes accountability. The more latitude you provide your team members, the more systems you'll need to employ to make sure they perform. Thus, Five-Star Bosses think out-of-the-box to come up with creative ways that accomplish the goals and help people succeed.

As you can see, many of these theories and models overlap. In terms of Job Fit, it offers the potential to increase satisfaction and decrease dissatisfaction (Herzberg). Another benefit is that it improves the likelihood of success. The research on job satisfaction is interesting. The common thought is that the more satisfied people are at work, the better they'll perform. That's why so many companies do satisfaction surveys. Yet the research supporting this is not strong. Studies note there is a much stronger connection between performance and satisfaction, meaning that the better we perform, the more satisfied we'll be. So instead of trying to increase satisfaction so people will perform better, Five-Star Bosses put more emphasis on helping them perform better, knowing that it will result in higher satisfaction. That means we want to hire and train for the position. When training is seen as optional or even a perk, we underestimate its importance and aren't leveraging the research in the field of performance and motivation.

This is the first of our two chapters on motivation, but before we move forward, let's push pause to unpack this content a bit. That's important to do when you're training, so as not to overwhelm your people and underestimate the problem of information overload.

Five-Star Boss Questions:

1. Name two or three aha's you got from this chapter.
2. Which of these theories did you find most intriguing and why?
3. What are two or three motivational issues facing your current work environment?
4. What specifically could you do to apply these to your work?
5. Which of these theories have you seen done effectively in work environments?

Chapter 14

Motivational Strategies, Take Two

More About Moving People

Here are more key motivation theories that Five-Star Bosses understand.

Goal Setting

One of the most utilized motivation theories is goal setting. This may seem like common sense, but it actually is a distinct theory that includes research on how to establish goals effectively. In this skinny description, let me call out three interesting findings in the research. An underlying assumption is that you'll make sure the goal supports the objectives, namely what you want the outcome to be. Managing by objectives (MBO) is a strategic approach to running a team and an organization.

The first recommendation is to utilize the SMART model. Five-Star Bosses make sure goals are Specific, Measurable, Achievable, Relevant, and Time-bound (SMART). This is a great tool you can use for your planning meetings, weekly-monthly-quarterly-annual staff member goals, and of course for personal use. For example, you could ask your team to develop three to five SMART goals for this coming month, things they want to complete by the end of the month. You could do the same thing with the entire team, using a whiteboard to clarify each of the five elements. If someone says, "Improving our sales revenue by 10%," questions might follow:

- Is the 10% total or in a specific product or service (specific)?
- Is 10% realistic when we've been in negative growth during this recession (achievable)?
- Should our focus be on increasing sales at the moment when we have holes in our supply chain (relevant)?

You might be wondering, but what if the goal is attitudinal, such as "We want to improve our customer service"? Scientists say, "If it exists, it can be measured." True, it's often easier said than done. But in this case, you could create a goal that complaints will be reduced by 25% (measured) this quarter (time-bound). Assuming you have a way of recording complaints, this could work. If you do not, an example of a metric could be a 10-question online survey using a 1- to 5-scale for each question, resulting in a numerical average, for a minimum of 100 customers (you may need to incentivize them to complete it). Compare the numbers from the end of one quarter (baseline) to the end of the next quarter (comparison). These are examples of how you might use this, but obviously applied to your context.

A second goal-setting principle Five-Star Bosses utilize is participation. Research shows that people are more committed to goals they help develop. A lot of companies establish goal setting as a top-down process, whereby bosses set the goals for teams and announce them in monthly or quarterly meetings. Team members raise their eyebrows, roll their eyes, and mutter, "You've got to be kidding." This is flawed motivationally because you're creating renters instead of owners. Let me explain. We used to live in Monterey, California, a beautiful town on the coast about 100 miles south of San Francisco. Monterey is an eclectic community with a mix of education, tourism, military, and agriculture industries. We lived in a neighborhood just above downtown, where locals lived along with a high percent of military and students who rented. In the evenings, my wife and I walked through the neighborhoods. Sometimes we played a game, "Renter or Owner?" We tried to guess if the occupants rented their homes or owned them, based on how the home was maintained. The basic premise is that owners take more pride in their property and keep it looking nice, whereas renters don't care as much, thus don't keep them as neat and tidy. Obviously it's a bit of a stereotype, because at the time we were renting and kept our home nice, paying for things like landscaping out of our own pocket. The same is true of cars. People typically drive rented cars harder than they do their own. The tendency is true that we're generally more committed to what we own and develop than what we rent.

Here's the point. Do whatever you can to involve your team members in the development of goals they'll be charged to reach. With this comes improved commitment, engagement, and performance. Naturally you'll want to be involved, partly because you want to make sure they align with your team's objectives, but also to ensure they're sufficiently challenging. Some will set too low of goals because they want to make sure they reach them. Others will set unrealistically high goals, unlikely to achieve them. Research shows that when the manager is involved with the team member, goal quality improves. The point is that participation in individual, team, and larger change plans are great ways to increase motivation.

A third thing Five-Star Bosses do is find the Goldilocks standard. In the story of Goldilocks and the Three Bears, the little girl wanders into the animals' house and finds a bed that's too hard, too soft, and just right. Five-Star Bosses figure out what constitutes just-right goals, challenging but not too challenging. Research shows that people experience elevated motivation when the goal is not too soft and not too hard. Easy goals don't bring out the best in our team. But when companies establish too high of goals, this has an even more extreme effect on motivation than setting easy ones. The trick is figuring out how to increase performance without pushing too hard. The other challenge comes when you're establishing individual goals, because all your people are not the same in terms of talent, drive, and experience. This is where knowing your team and your business comes into play.

Stretch goals are unique, short-term opportunities to give your team members challenging goals to see how well they perform. They can be a result of conditions that require a more demanding response in your company or proactive goals that the manager sets for the purpose of seeing if an employee has what it takes to perform at a higher level. Another time to implement a stretch goal is when you're on a plateau or you sense that status quo and monotony are occurring. Stretch goals should not be over-used, so that you end up burning out team members. It's the equivalent of a runner giving the last kick before crossing the finish line, and "leaving it all on the court" as they say in basketball. Everyone needs situations that push oneself and raise performance to the next level. If someone cannot do that, it's helpful to know as a Five-Star Boss because you don't want to overwhelm team members and set them up for failure. This can reveal who is and is not ready for a promotion.

Responses to Dissatisfaction

Another helpful motivation theory for Five-Star Bosses involves understanding how people respond to dissatisfaction in the workplace. (This is more of a general dissatisfaction versus Herzberg's Two-Factor Model.) Although we might think that dissatisfied people ultimately quit their jobs, many do not. There are four common ways that people express their disappointments. Let me unpack the following graph for you so you can better understand how people behave when they're not happy at work.

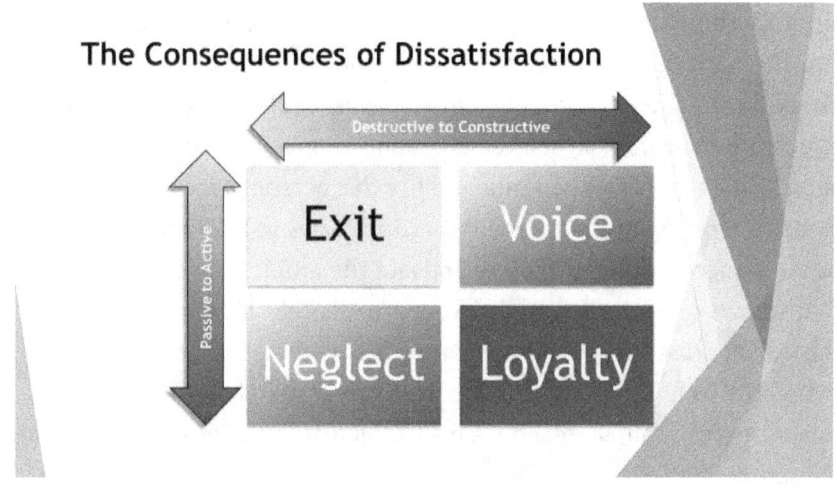

Exit: The logical response for people who are dissatisfied at work is to leave. This employee tends to be self-motivated and instead of trying to improve the situation, he decides to seek alternative employment. There's not much you can do about these people, unless you do the "stay interviews" designed to retain your best talent. Being proactive can help you avoid losing quality people. One of my two career regrets is leaving a job I had as a young adult to pursue my graduate degree. My boss could have kept me if he'd sat down with me to discuss what it would take to keep me. I could have done a grad degree nearby while staying employed. I hadn't considered that option, so by the time we made our announcement, our decision was cemented.

Voice: This response is proactive, desiring to help improve the work environment so the employee can stay. Although some managers perceive these people as trouble-makers, in reality the employees are striving to make things better. When insecure managers respond negatively to these suggestions, they alienate the employees, increasing the likelihood they will leave. Five-Star Bosses understand that this is an opportunity to listen and possibly respond to the employee's desires, to keep good talent and move the organization forward.

Neglect: This response treats work as merely a paycheck. The goal is to stay off management's radar, doing the minimum required to retain employment and finding fulfillment elsewhere. Changing this attitude is affected by the work structure. For example, in a union or government agency, managers can't do much to fire this person. It's better to sit and listen to the employee and see if there are ways to improve performance and shape a job to activate the employee's inner motivation. According to statistics, approximately 2/3 of employees in the U.S. are disengaged, meaning they are working but not highly motivated to bring their best. Five-Star Bosses do what they can to minimize this negative response by listening and improving accountability.

Loyalty: The fourth response includes employees who are dissatisfied but still loyal. The dream of these people is that the organization will become more responsive and change for the better. The goal of the Five-Star Boss is to affirm the team member's loyalty, to stick it out yet not assume that physical presence is the same as emotional engagement. Companies often assume that everything is hunky dory, when in reality the employee is hoping for improvement. Five-Star Bosses don't assume that a lack of complaining is the same as engagement. Rather, they proactively pursue the ideas and concerns of the quieter team members who may actually be dissatisfied but hoping for improvement.

Justice Theories

One of the most important recent themes in organizations that impacts motivation involves justice, equity, and fairness. People have become highly sensitive in recent years to real and perceived conditions of favoritism, sexism, sexual harassment, prejudice, bigotry, and other forms of inequity. Starbucks shut down all of its stores in the middle of the day to do sensitivity training because a single store manager called the police on two minority males who required them to leave for loitering. The Me Too movement resulted in the firings of dozens of executives, as women (primarily) voiced their anger at objectification and workplace harassment. As I write this book, the university where I teach (USC) is one of those included in the scandal of wealthy parents paying bribes to get their children accepted into elite schools.

Text, Tweets, emails, and cell phone recordings posted on social media have become a means for weighing the worth of a political candidate, entertainer, executive, and the everyday manager. The bottom line is that it is affecting the bottom line of numerous companies. The uproar over the unfairness of people with power gaining advantage over those with less is at times deafening. Tangible results include firings, fines, jail time, stock price decreases, and dissolving companies. My point is not to argue for or against this cultural sensitivity, but rather to note that Five-Star Bosses read the context in which they work and learn to respond appropriately. Following is an introduction of three sub-categories in the Justice Theories bucket to help you understand what may impact the motivation of your people and help you avoid undue conflict and political implosion.

Distributive Justice: This has to do with how rewards are distributed in an organization. People want to know that they're receiving their fair share. For example, are you paying women at the same rate as men? Do you cater to older people more than younger people, or visa versa? Do you offer the same opportunities for pay, perks, rewards, training, and promotions regardless of demographics like age, gender, race, or personality? Some companies, such as Whole Foods, support "open book" policies where everyone can see what employees earn. Most companies shudder to think of this because of variances in their salaries.

Procedural Justice: This focuses on processes, meaning is there fairness in how things are done? For example, if I have a complaint regarding a boss or policy, can I raise this without being punished? Does everyone have an opportunity to tug at the boss's ear, or is it only for his or her favorites? Is everyone given the same rights to be considered for promotions, or are there unfair practices so that some are offered better opportunities? Procedural issues relate to how things get done, communication, processes, and polity equity.

Interactional Justice: This focuses on how people are treated in relationships. Is everyone honored and esteemed? A Five-Star Boss understands that if people think he or she has favorites who get the best shifts and roles, they'll be upset and less motivated to work. When there is a real or perceived difference in how certain team members are recognized, this will upset people and impact their performance. Obviously, a perceived disregard in any of these three areas will decrease motivation. A perceived regard will primarily increase commitment, directly connected to motivation.

These motivational strategies, based on enduring theories and research in the field, will help you improve your ability to move your team effectively. So while everyone possesses free will and can thwart even the best leader's encouragement, Five-Star Bosses are more productive in bringing out the best in people. Over the long haul, this results in cumulatively far more positive results.

Five-Star Boss Questions:

1. Which of these theories did you find most intriguing?
2. How can you apply these to your work environment?
3. Why do you think managers so frequently struggle with motivation issues?
4. What are things you'd do right away to improve the motivation in your organization?
5. How can you do this as a manager and/or who could make some of these changes?

Chapter 15

There's a U in Team

Creating Synergy Among Your Members

The DNA of Organizations

DNA has transformed the way forensic investigators discover who performed crimes decades after they're committed and classified as cold cases. The reason is that every remnant of skin, saliva, and body fluids contains the genetic code of a person. So while you may not be the CEO of a company with 50,000 employees, your team of five has the DNA of your larger organization in it. If you want to be a part of changing your company, you need to focus on creating the best team possible. As you improve your team, you'll be adding value to the larger organization and as a result, you'll be considered a valuable asset by those with greater power than you. Thus, you're a gene donor for your organization.

One of the most important things you can do to create a strong team is understand the phases it goes through. In 1965, Bruce Tuckman introduced a four-stage model of group development that has become a staple among those who help develop teams. Since then, a fifth stage has been added for a more complete picture. Each stage is developmental and sequential, yet not static. That means a team that gets to stage three can return to stage two. Teams can also get stuck in a stage, requiring a special impetus to progress.

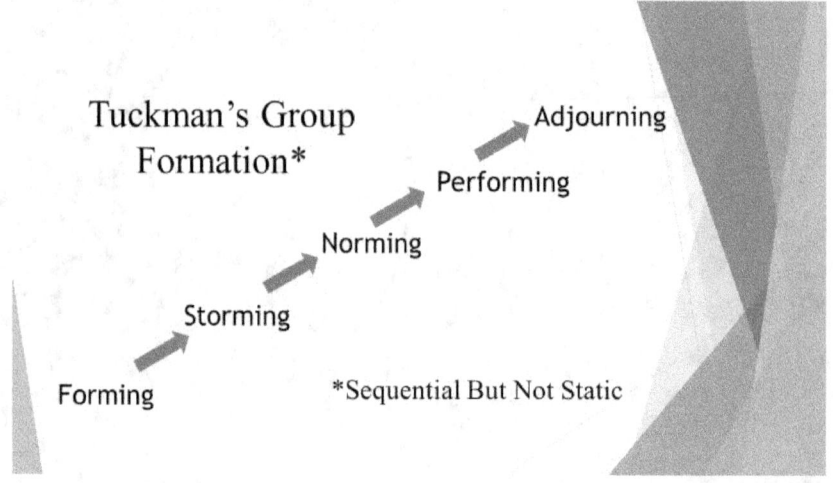

The first phase of a team is *Forming*, the initial stage when team members meet, get to know each other's personalities, and begin bonding. At this point everyone is pretty much a stranger, at least in terms of a common goal. The members aren't necessarily clear what their purpose is or what their role will be in the team. They are trying to gain guidance regarding their direction. They come to the team with a perception of what is going to be required, but they don't necessarily agree on how they're going to accomplish it and what the team is going to become.

The second phase of a team is *Storming*, a season of potential conflict created by a variety of conditions. The first condition is a lack of clarity as to the purpose of the team. When leadership hasn't clarified the purpose of the group, each member comes in with his or her own assumptions. Another condition for conflict is pre-established personality issues. People who know each other before serving on a team often bring their past experiences, good and bad, that can impact a team. Research shows that having some pre-established relationships can increase collaboration. Naturally, bad blood between team members can reduce it. Perhaps the most common condition to predict thunder is jostling for power and influence, primarily as it relates to roles; namely, who is going to do what. Recognizing this natural and normal phase won't discourage a good team leader.

The third phase of a team is *Norming*, the stage when team members clarify their individual roles along with establishing team process and procedures. This is where responsibilities are identified and assigned. These can be simple things such as sharing contact info and determining preferred communication to use (i.e. texting, email, Zoom, Skype, face to face). Other items include how often and how long you'll meet, how important punctuality is, and the importance of hitting deadlines on time. Think of your team as a family. One or both parents would set the rules regarding eating at meals, curfew, TV watching, and chores. As adults, you don't want to come across as paternal, but you do want to make sure everyone is familiar with the "house rules" to avoid frustrations (moving you back to the Storming). Often, these norms are unwritten and unspoken. You know this because when someone ignores the norm (i.e. punctuality), team members get frustrated. Thus, it's often good as a team leader to go over little expectations that you may think should be common knowledge, in case some people are assuming different things than you.

The fourth phase of a team is *Performing*, the stage when you begin seeing the team synergize and become productive. The power of performing is that it tends to motivate the team members. They enjoy each other more as they see the results of their collaboration. This is a good time for managers to affirm the team and compliment them for working together. When performance falls off for some reason, this is when you'll need to troubleshoot, which can move you back to the Norming stage ("Hey, Sarah, you're not hitting your deadlines") or even Storming ("John's trying to do my job again."). Teams want feedback to know how they're doing and, within reason, how to achieve even more.

A healthy team can go on for a long time, but eventually a time will come when it will need to end. This leads to the fifth stage, *Adjourning*. The purpose of this stage is to say goodbye and bring closure to the team. Temporary teams may celebrate with something as little as a "thank you for your time and effort" note. Long-term teams and those that have sacrificed a lot should have a bigger farewell and celebration. The opportunity to offer applause, call out members who performed exceptionally, and allow opportunities for members to affirm one another are all ideas to make this stage effective. An effective manager will be sensitive to emotions of sadness if the team bonded and mourns the loss of comradery. Navy SEALs state that the saddest day in their lives is the day they leave their team of brothers with whom they faced deadly situations over the years.

Creating Cohesion

Cohesion is how close and tight-knit a team is. Think of it as the glue. Some teams are like Super Glue. They are stuck on each other. Others are like Post-It notes, requiring little pressure to peel them away from each other. The reason Navy SEALs feel such pain in the Adjourning stage is their cohesion. Many admit that they feel closer to their brothers than their own family members. This is because of their elite status, the life and death situations they experience together, and the incredible closeness you gain when you interact so often and achieve so much together. As you'll see in a moment, these are the ingredients for strong cohesion.

The downside of a cohesive team is that you begin thinking you're better than you are and begin separating from the larger organization. Highly bonded groups are more vulnerable to the dangers of groupthink (see Chapter 8, Decision-Making Blind Spots). Highly cohesive groups also are more difficult to break into, so that new members feel alienated and thus fail to bond with the larger group. Tight-knit groups aren't always more productive, such as when they begin prioritizing having fun together over focusing on work. For example, you may have a highly cohesive warehouse team that wastes time goofing around, playing practical jokes on each other and ignoring goals. Thus, Five-Star Bosses build cohesive teams but also maintain a balance.

Research shows that the following factors impact how a team bonds:

- High selection criteria: The more difficult it is to get on the team, the more likely they'll feel special and united, so don't make it sound like you're desperate or simply looking for warm bodies.
- Size: Smaller teams tend to be more cohesive than larger ones. The rule of thumb is to stay under double digits (10) if possible, and only have as many people as you need to cover the bases.
- Similarity among team members: Too much diversity can reduce cohesion, although diverse qualities vary in their impact.
- Member interaction: Teams feel closer when they get together, talk, and work together, so do what you can to maintain a sense of community.
- External challenges: When a team experiences opposition and difficulties from outside of it (versus internal conflict), it is more likely to be tighter. "It's us against them!"
- Success: When teams experience victory together, they tend to bond more, so when possible, create some wins and celebrations as soon as you're able.

Be a Thermostat, Not a Thermometer

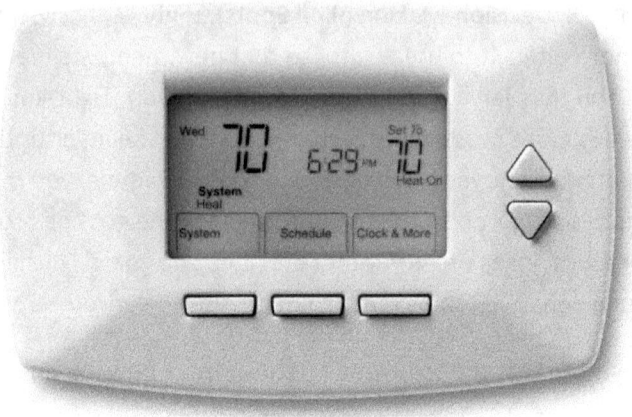

When you walk into a room, chances are you'll see a device on the wall that reads the temperature and also sets the temperature. A thermometer tells the temperature, but the thermostat sets it. As the Boss of your team, you're a thermostat. Your team members take cues from you regarding their work attitude, whether or not they want to be on your team, and how you perceive functioning together. The most important single factor of a team is the attitude the team leader sets for it. If you want it to be cold and frigid or warm and comfortable, you establish it. This is what we call climate—the emotional status and level of comfort on a team and in an office.

As the Boss, you determine the culture of your team. Even in a great organization, some teams are dysfunctional and divided. Yet in lousy organizations, some teams buck the trend and emerge as strong and cohesive. The biggest single factor of these differences is not the members or the task or the mission of the company, but rather the ability of the team leader to create a dynamic environment. So while it's a heavy burden to be a Five-Star Boss, it's also an exciting challenge to help your team unify and enjoy working together. Making the most of the people and opportunities you've been given is what your role is all about. Blaming others and making excuses for lackluster performance is code for "I can't do it. I don't have what it takes." If your team isn't where you want it to be, keep doing the best with what you've got. Apply other principles in this book to establish a cohesive team.

Five-Star Boss Questions:

1. What Stage do you think your current team is in?
2. Describe behaviors you've seen in the Storming Stage.
3. How would you explain the "norms" of your team?
4. What are the stated or assumed behaviors and practices your members expect of each other?
5. What are ways you can become a better thermostat for your team?

THE FIVE-STAR BOSS

Chapter 16
Handling the Heat
Managing Sparks w/o Burning Down the Office

When Sparks Fly

In November 2018, we received a mandatory evacuation notification to leave our home. The Hill Fire that eventually charred over 6,000 acres in Ventura County was less than 4 miles from our house. At the same time, about 6 miles in the opposite direction, the Woolsey fire was devastating over 100,000 acres from Oak Park to Malibu. After the roads reopened, my wife and I drove through Malibu Canyon and up Pacific Coast Highway to view the carnage of hundreds of homes and what looked like a black lunar landscape. White nylon fences surrounding property lines melted from the intense heat, looking like Dali's *The Persistence of Memory* painting with drooping clocks. Homes, vineyards, stables, palm trees, and automobiles continued to smolder after firefighters doused them with water and chemicals. Many of the flames were extinguished as they fanned into the waves of the Pacific Ocean. This catastrophic damage resulted from tiny sparks that ignited some of the worst fires in California history.

No doubt, one of the most strenuous issues related to being a boss is managing the flames of conflict. When you talk about conflict to most people, they shudder. It's seen as a negative thing. The reason is that it's rarely handled well. Like Pavlov's dog that salivates when a bell rings because it's conditioned to connect the sound of the bell with food, most have endured pain related to conflict because it is rarely managed well.

One of the aha moments many in my organizational behavior class experience is when they learn that conflict can be good. There's a difference between functional and dysfunctional conflict. Functional conflict happens when people share divergent opinions that result in better ideas, clearer communication, and enhanced commitment to a project. Once I worked for a wonderful organization that hired consultants so it could improve. One of their findings was that the company lacked sufficient conflict. The "Best Place to Work" winning company confused peace with prosperity. Sometimes performance suffers when people don't wrestle over different ideas. When idea-sharing decreases because people fear hurting feelings, even good companies can suffer.

One technique to avoid this is to designate a "Devil's Advocate," someone whose official role is to raise contrary ides such as, "But what if the supply chain gets interrupted and we can't ship on time?" By passing around this responsibility, you help those who tend to be contrarians by nature avoid getting labeled as killjoys and pessimists. "John, today you're the Devil's Advocate, so it's your job to come up with logical concerns and potential problems during our discussions to make sure we're not missing something." This incorporates critical thinking, where you consider both benefits and risks of all potential solutions.

Yet a lot of conflict isn't functional because it focuses on personalities instead of problems and egos instead of issues. When conflict becomes relational, it is the boss's responsibility to rein it in. I have an entire class on conflict resolution that I teach for business majors, so know there are some great books on this topic if you want to go deeper. Following is a model that offers five styles to manage conflict. Each has unique strengths and weaknesses, meaning that your goal is to use the right tool in the appropriate situation. Although most rely on one or two of these a majority of the time, the Five-Star Boss keeps all five tools in her toolbox to apply when needed.

Competing: This is also known as directing and dominating, when a person quickly makes a decision that may not be popular with others. The benefits of this style are that it's quick in case of an emergency and effective when an issue is liable to blow up with too much time spent in discussing it. It also works if you have a big personality who'll take advantage of noncompetitive actions. In spite of the positive options, the number of conditions where this works well is limited. The risks of this style are that you'll be seen as intimidating and limited in leadership ability, if used too often. You'll also shut down creativity and foster a sense of fear among your team members. While you may get compliance, you'll lower commitment. Many new bosses resort to this mode because they confuse being a boss with acting bossy.

Collaborating: This style is commonly known as problem solving, as it integrates different ideas and is likely to increase acceptance by those involved. The goal is to merge the insights from various perspectives. It's the most effective approach to begin each conflict session, because it focuses on learning. We raised three sons, and my wife was brilliant at this approach (while I tended to overuse the Competing style). She'd sit the boys down and ask each one for his perspective of the situation, sometimes separately, at other times together. Collaborating begins by asking, "What's the problem we need to solve?" Sometimes you discover that both parties involved want the same thing, but misunderstood each other. The strength of this style is that it focuses on facts and open, healthy communication. It becomes a mystery to solve or a puzzle to complete. The risk of Collaborating is that it can take a lot of time and energy to go through the process. It also requires strong facilitation skills and patience of those involved.

Compromising: Think of avoidance here as an intentional choice, not ignoring responsibility or hiding. This style works best when you don't have sufficient time to Collaborate. Therefore, it's a good back-up plan for the problem-solving approach. It's also beneficial when parties with equivalent power have mutually exclusive needs, meaning there's little chance they'll be able to resolve the issue. By helping each give in and give up something valuable to them, they're more apt to feel that the process is equitable and fair. While no one likes to give up part of what they want, a lack of fairness will result in parties being upset and will likely decrease motivation.

Avoiding: This style is effective when there are more pressing matters, when the issue is trivial, and when there's little chance in resolving the conflict. Sometimes it makes the most sense not to pursue issues because the process itself can make it seem more important than it is.

It's also helpful when people need to cool down and gain their composure and perhaps do some research. Time to gain more info allows you or others to learn more of the facts. The risk of avoiding is that if you use it too often, it will frustrate people and make them think you're out of touch. Failing to deal with the issue can make matters worse. Like an untreated infection can harm the body, an unresolved conflict can fester in a team.

Accommodating: This style is also referred to as obliging, where you give in to help resolve the situation. This is beneficial when you realize you're wrong, so the other party sees you as being reasonable, humble, and secure. It's also effective when the relationship is at risk of deteriorating, making that more important than the issue. Sometimes you give in to keep the peace. It's also a way to earn social credits. This happens a lot in politics, where one person gives in on an issue so that the next time, the other person concedes. The risks of accommodating are that people will take advantage of you if you do it too often and you won't be respected as a strong leader who stands for what is right.

Delivery Mode Selection

Before we leave this dynamic topic, let me offer some wisdom regarding how, when, and where to confront. Five-Star Bosses understand that as important as conflict management styles are, choosing the right setting is essential—talking to an employee in his workspace, avoiding group settings, and avoiding times when people are tired or emotionally trained. But one of the most common mistakes bosses make in managing conflict involves the type of medium they use.

If you want a confrontational message to result in unnecessary damage, then convey it with text, email, or memo. Here's why. Think of message channels as pipes. A small pipe, like the one under your sink at home, can only transmit a certain amount of water in a set amount of time. When you flush your toilet, it can handle a much larger volume because the pipe is much larger. The diameter of the pipes transferring water from the lake or water tower of your city are significantly larger. Now, think of a message like water. If you have a thick, rich message, it requires a higher capacity "pipe" or means to transfer it. A face-to-face meeting is a rich medium, meaning you can send and receive a high volume of information, such as non-verbal gestures and intonation, and allow for immediate feedback and clarification. A lean medium, like a text, email, or memo, simply doesn't have the capacity to deliver rich messages. That's why they get stuck in the pipe.

We've all read about significant others who break up with their partners with a text. We grimace when we think of that because it seems so insensitive. During World War II, "Dear John" letters were the equivalent, when a girlfriend broke up with her soldier boyfriend while he was overseas in battle. Here's the big point: never confront a person or convey a conflict message electronically. Chances are very high it will come back to bite you and undermine your relationship with the other person. If you can't do a face-to-face, then set up a conference call. If you can't see the other person, then set up a phone appointment. It is more efficient, but more importantly, more effective.

After every semester, I usually have a couple of students who want to know why they got the grade they did in my class; most of the topics I teach involve subjective grading, since they deal with organizational behavior and leadership, which are inexact topics. Last semester, I had a student who emailed me his disdain for the grade he received, even though I explained the process to the entire class. I offered him specifics on his grade and then said, "If you have further questions, let's set up a phone appointment." He was upset because he got a B, and needed a B+ so that he could go on an international trip with the college. Apparently, he didn't do well in other classes, because a B-average wouldn't have kept him from studying abroad. Regardless, I was sensitive to his situation, but confirmed where his score was compared with his colleagues' scores. Despite my suggestion to call me, he continued to email, asking me two more times for more details and explanations on his final grade.

Each time I politely responded, "As I said before, let's set up a phone appointment instead of sending so many emails." He never called me, choosing to hide behind his keyboard. I never told him this, but I was prepared to reconsider his grade if he had a strong explanation as to why this grade change would legitimately keep him from studying abroad. I needed to hear more of the story. He needed to sell me. But since he never called, he retained his B in the class. In today's culture, more and more people hide behind Tweets, emails, and social media posts instead of looking in the eyes of the person they're upset with and trying to resolve the issue. Five-Star Bosses select the right medium for the type of message they want to send.

Functional conflict helps your team be great. Dysfunctional conflict will grate your team to pieces. Firefighters often prevent catastrophes by causing intentional burns, thus removing fuel. Five-Star Bosses manage conflict by using it to develop, not destroy, team performance. They do this by assessing the situation and then applying the best tool to resolve the issue.

Five-Star Boss Questions:

1. What is your preferred conflict management style(s)?
2. Describe a situation in your organization where each of the styles would be most appropriate.
3. Describe an example of where someone selected the wrong conflict management style that ended poorly.
4. What is your superior's preferred conflict management style?
5. What can you do to manage the conflict better on your team?

Chapter 17

Competent Jerks

& Other Team Members

The Four People on Teams

Nearly all team members can be plotted on the two qualities we just discussed, competence (performance) and compassion (interpersonal skills). We've all known bosses, colleagues, and team members who seemed intelligent and skilled but didn't give a rip about others. They were offensive, rubbed people the wrong way, and didn't seem to care about relationships. If we had to choose between working around a person who is competent but uncaring and an individual who was incompetent yet caring, who do you think most would prefer? The research clearly shows that people value compassion over competence. Most would rather work with someone who was nice to be around and not that effective than someone who was very talented and offensive. Let's apply the principles we discussed in Chapter 6 to the people on your team.

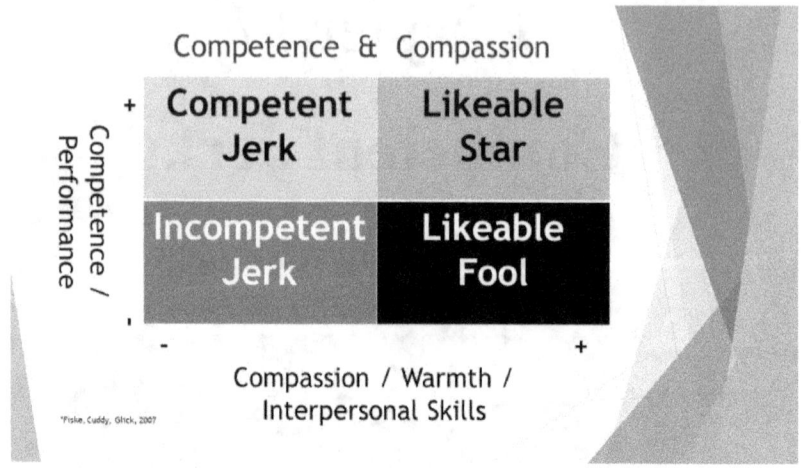

The Incompetent Jerk: We'll begin in the lower left-hand corner and work counter-clockwise, so that we end with the most challenging member on teams. The Incompetent Jerk is a person who either doesn't apply himself intentionally or doesn't have the capacity to perform in his current role. At the same time, his people skills really stink because he either lacks social intelligence or he just doesn't try. This person is a big drag to your team and at least a small drag to your organization. While most companies can't just fire someone for these issues, you definitely want to build a file on this person so that you can let him go as soon as possible. In the meantime, you need to put him on a performance improvement plan (PIP) ASAP. Chances are this person has already ostracized himself from the rest of the group, who's tired of carrying his dead weight and weary of his lousy attitude. If you fail to remove this person as soon as possible, the rest of the team will conclude that you don't "get it" or have the fortitude to manage well.

The Likeable Fool: To the right of the Incompetent Jerk is the gregarious, fun-loving people person who just doesn't seem to have the skill set required to get much done. Often, this person gets hired and/or promoted because of her exceptional interpersonal skills, but then everyone discovers that she over-sold herself; she's in over her head. This person is worth keeping around, as long as you can help her get the needed training to function well in her role or perhaps assign her to tasks within her skill set. People skills are more difficult to teach than technical skills, so providing a clear accountability plan with support and training may fix the problem.

The Likeable Star: In the upper right-hand corner is the truly amazing team member. This person is not only good in his tasks, he's also wonderful to be around. His infectious people skills, whether quiet or outgoing, make people want to be around him. Your strategy for this person is keeping him on the team. Five-Star Bosses know that if they put all their attention on putting out fires and focusing on lower performers, Likeable Stars will often find more interesting roles on other teams or begin getting bored. This is the proverbial good child who goes bad when the parents are focusing so much attention on the troublemakers.

Offer quarterly or semi-annual "stay" interviews, the opposite of an exit interview after someone resigns. "John, you're doing amazing work. What do we need to do to keep you on our team? Where would you like to be in 1-3 years from now? Are there any other roles or tasks you'd like to go after in our division?" These types of questions, every 3-6 months, can help you retain the caliber of talent that makes a team great. Five-Star Bosses invest more time in keeping their high performers happy than in keeping lower performers from being crappy.

The Competent Jerk: Finally, let's talk about the elephant in the room: the high performing team member who most don't like. Research shows that when people have to choose between working with a Competent Jerk or a Likeable Fool, most prefer the fool. The reason is that someone who is really smart and highly talented yet lacks social intelligence makes work irritating. This person is likely to rub people the wrong way to the point that they begin quitting. The problem is that this person is so good at what she does that she's difficult to let go. The ineffective manager lets this person get away with things simply because she's such a great performer and, well, she turns in the numbers (whatever that means in your setting). But at the end of the day, this person is doing more damage than you realize. The Competent Jerk is diminishing your team's cohesion, thus reducing its effectiveness and alienating other performers.

The best strategy to mitigate the relational cost of a Competent Jerk is to sequester her as much as possible from the others. She is toxic to a team. At the same time, outline a plan that specifically addresses actions she can take to improve her social skills. Help her see the impact her words and actions have on others. If you have resources, offer to hire a coach or talk to HR to explore ideas. Sometimes you can redeem a Competent Jerk or at least lower the negative impact. Yet, more often than not, you have to end up getting the person off your team. Most of the time, her influence on others will not offset the strong performance gained.

Although you may not recognize each of these four people on your current team, no doubt you will eventually. Your ability to develop people and help your team work together is your primary job as a Five-Star Boss. Although you'll find individuals who straddle the line between the between cells, usually you'll be able to place them in a specific quadrant. You'll want to create intentional development plans for each person to help them reach their potential as well as create synergy on the team. Your inability to do this will decrease your credibility as a leader, resulting in fewer rewards and promotions, and more headaches.

Five-Star Boss Questions:

1. List the people on your team and place each person in one of the four cells.
2. Create a simple development plan for each person based on the advice in this chapter.
3. How would you rate yourself based on this model?
4. If you were your supervisor, what would you recognize for your development?
5. Who can you trust in your organization who knows your team and can help you analyze your members according to this model?

*Fiske, S., Cuddy, A., & Glick, P (2007). Universal dimensions of social cognition: Warmth and competence. *Trends in Cognitive Sciences, 11*, 77-83 and Casiaro & Lobo (2005).

Chapter 18
EI, EI, Oh!

Farming Emotional Intelligence

Defining "EI"

The above family photo is a lot like a typical company team. Most include members who are social-emotionally more mature (adults) and less (kids). Regardless of gender or date of birth, team members project varying abilities in responding to circumstances. Kids (less mature adults) are not as self-aware or able to handle what is going on inside of them. You'll have a few emotional adolescents (sometimes adults;

sometimes children) and a number of adults (more mature). Five-Star Bosses fill a parental role (mature), being patient with their family members while helping them grow up.

The photo of the family above was no doubt taken on a good day when everything seemed to be going well. A corporate example is the company website, with clearly defined mission, smiling employees, and proud, grinning bosses. But those of us who are parents realize that everyone's not smiling all the time. The ability to identify and manage emotions is referred to as emotional intelligence (EI). This is one of the most important things bosses do, because we are in the people business. We all know those unaware of what's going on inside of them, let alone able to manage their emotions. These chains of events can disrupt productivity, team cohesion, and job satisfaction. No one likes working in an environment where people are on edge, gossiping, pouting, and assassinating character.

Peter Salovey and John D. Mayer coined the term "Emotional Intelligence" in 1990, using it to define social awareness, referring to how emotions influence relationships. A few years later, a psychologist named Daniel Goleman popularized the concept in a bestselling book on the topic. One of my favorite leadership books that I recommend you read (after you finish this book) is *Primal Leadership*. It's about EI for leaders. It's one of those books you want to put in a brown paper bag and leave in your supervisor's mailbox. We all know people who seem unaware of how they're coming across, affecting others adversely. In full disclosure, I've been that person more times than I'd like to admit. Perhaps you're one of them. If you want a good example of a low EI boss, watch a few reruns of The Office. Michael Scott is the comedic representative of a toxic boss. It's painfully funny. Perhaps the reason it's the most watched sitcom series is that we relate to the awkwardness of low EI people around us.

A person's social-emotional acumen affects how he functions as well as how the people around him function. Five-Star Bosses possess high EI and help their team members improve theirs. The good news, according to experts in the field, is that unlike IQ, personality, and any number of genetic-oriented talents and traits, EI can be developed. Here's a quick overview of the subject, because as a boss, your effectiveness will be impacted by your EI. The two pairs you need to understand are Awareness-Regulation and Self-Others. We'll explain these in the order of sequential development.

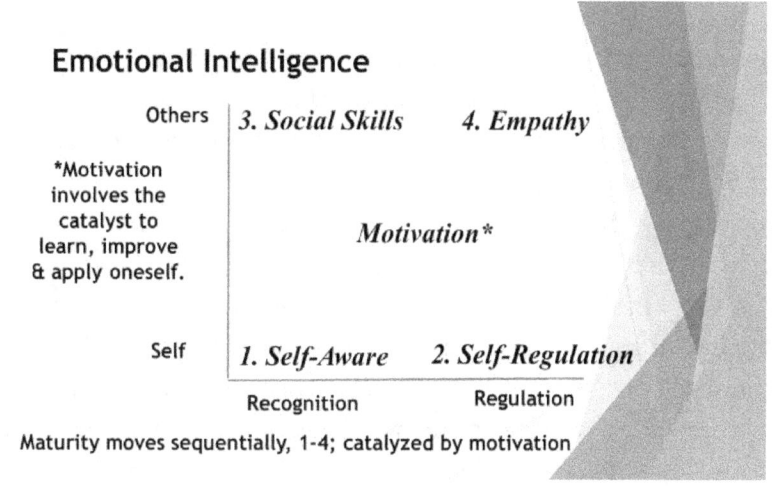

Self-Aware: EI begins with self-awareness. This pertains to a person's ability to understand what is going on inside of oneself. Is he sad or mad, satisfied or happy? Self-aware people are able to accurately articulate their feelings. Some are more attune than others. My mother, while even-keeled, had difficulty verbalizing her emotions. When I asked, "How are you feeling?" she was unsure. Other than describing how she felt physically, there seemed to be a separation between her emotions and ability to identify them. Counseling can improve one's ability to be in touch with emotions.

Self-Regulation: The next developmental stage involves the ability to manage emotion-based responses. It's one thing to be aware of a feeling, but it's another to keep it from triggering unhealthy responses to others. For example, road rage is the inability to control one's anger, resulting in reckless and often devastating behaviors. People with higher

EI recognize their escalating anger and then activate self-discipline, backing off and cooling down. This involves putting oneself in time-out. Because alcohol reduces inhibitions, it often causes people to do things they regret later because they respond to their current emotional state without regulation. Self-management is not about avoiding or not having emotions, but rather being able to override them to avoid destructive responses.

Social Skills: After a person is able to manage herself, she can then focus on others. Social skills provide a sense of what is going on inside of others. People with higher EI go beyond what another person is saying or doing; she listens to the pitch, rate of speech, and intonation. She looks at the other person's eyes, facial gestures, and other nonverbal cues. All of these provide input as she discerns the other person's state. Are they happy, anxious, frustrated, sad, feeling dismissed, aloof, or any number of other states of being? The ability to read people is a higher social skill. Five-Star Bosses don't just take things at face value. If they ask someone, "How are you doing?" and the person responds glibly, "Fine," that boss senses something may not be fine. Although she may not have time for an in-depth conversation in the hall, she will likely come back to the person later to see what's causing the team member's less-than-positive disposition. Perceiving tension between people is another example of demonstrating higher EI.

Empathy: People with a sense of what is going on inside others don't necessarily have the ability to help that person change his state. Perhaps you've heard a parent or boss say something like, "Oh just knock it off. Quit being such a baby." Not only does this not work, it can actually make the other person feel more frustrated. Empathy is considered the highest stage of EI. It's the ability to sense where people are emotionally and then help them get to a better state, by what you say or do.

My wife teaches her staff these types of skills because they interact with people experiencing degrees of dementia. For example, if a 90-year-old resident is agitated, wanting to leave because she thinks her parents are waiting for her at the bus stop, the natural reaction is to correct the delusion. "I'm sorry, Helen, but your parents aren't here anymore," or "No they're not, Helen. There isn't even a bus stop near here." But by teaching the care staff validation skills, they enter the senior's world. "I think the bus is running late today. What are you going to do when your parents pick you up?" This sort of conversation responds to the person where she is and then allows the talk to drift away from momentary emotions, de-escalating the agitation. Therapists are trained to use words and techniques that help their clients change their emotions and behaviors. People possessing high EI not only manage their own emotions but can create conditions that help others improve their own. People low in EI are unaware of how their responses can throw fuel on the fire, making matters worse. Again, go back to Michael Scott at Dunder Mifflin for more examples.

Motivation: A wild card on whether or not people mature is the issue of motivation. People who don't care what others think and are not interested in getting better usually don't. They struggle with social-emotional issues, perceiving it's the boss or the employees or the direct-reports, instead of looking in the mirror. Phrases such as "I've gotta be me" and "that's just the way I am" and "I'm just keeping it real" are often code for "I'm not that motivated to grow." Someone said, "I want to be like you when I grow up, but not too much like you." Someone else wrote, "You'll never forget him, at least not without a lot of therapy." Toxicity in the workplace is more a result of low EI than any other single issue. Bosses are the thermostats who set team temperature. When the boss is neurotic, no one's happy.

Growing EI

Hopefully you figured out that the title of this chapter is from the childhood song, "Old McDonald Had a Farm." It's a bit corny, but EI is a tool for growing your business and it's also something you can help hone on your team. Some of your people were likely raised by 30-year-old children, adults on the outside but kids on the inside. Their parents lacked social-emotional maturity, growing up on an emotional roller coaster. They were screamed at, neglected, and perhaps physically abused. Unfortunately, becoming a parent doesn't require a license or certification, so all kinds of people become one. As a boss, you inherit team members with a variety of family of origin issues, some of which will impact their performance in the office. But as their boss, the best thing you can do to help them is increase your own EI. Here are some quick ideas for how to do that.

- *Find a coach*: A coach could be a professional counselor or an executive coach. Find a person with whom you can share situations and who can then guide you through the process, not so much by telling you what to do as much as asking strategic questions to help you begin thinking differently about more effective ways of responding.
- *Develop a mental mentor*: We have a chapter on finding a mentor, but in this sense, it may be as simple as thinking about someone you know who handles their emotions well. Three people in my life include a former mentor, my wife, and one of our sons. The last one might surprise you, but one of our sons is mellow and handles people well, not getting upset or flustered. The goal of a mental mentor is to imagine how that person would respond in this situation. This allows us to get out of our own psyche by visualizing another person, offering cues we can follow.
- *Ask for accountability*: If you're working on a specific issue, let's say patience, find a confidante such as a friend, admin, or colleague to whom you give permission to raise the issue when appropriate. If you're willing, you could even bring it up with your team. "Hey, I know that sometimes in the middle of a discussion, I can become a bit impatient. For the next month, if it seems I'm coming across that way in a meeting, feel free to let me know or maybe we can come up with a signal, because I want to make sure my impatience isn't intimidating anyone or inhibiting our discussions." That's a gutsy move, but it also offers a good model to your team that will most likely raise their respect for you.

- *Embrace feedback*: You can ask for feedback from team members, colleagues, your superior, or even a spouse or significant other. Make sure you're in the frame of mind to hear it, but ask them straight on for ideas to improve or situations where you could have been more effective with a different approach. Naturally, if you have a history of rejecting feedback, it may be difficult for someone to trust you. A lot of people no longer participate in surveys or answer 360 feedback questions because it didn't do any good, or worse, it came back to bite them.
- *Read and learn*: Between the number of books, articles, webinars, and TED Talks, there are an array of resources to elevate your understanding of EI. Writing examples in a journal and then coming up with more effective responses, creating "do-overs" in your mind, help rehearse how you'll do better next time. EI can be grown, although some of us have more difficult soil than others.

Crucial Conversations

The authors of *Crucial Conversations: Tools for Talking When Stakes Are High* studied what it was that made certain people more effective than others. They discovered that Five-Star Bosses are especially good at facilitating critical discussions at key times. This is correlated to an individual's emotional maturity. Few things challenge EI more than intervening with people expressing opposing opinions in an emotionally charged environment, when a lot is at stake. The boss's ability to discern situations like these and handle them well requires sufficient EI and negotiation skills. Navigating situations like these offers unique opportunities to gain and lose respect as a boss, along with moving your team forward or setting it back. As we mentioned in the managing conflict chapter, issues that remain unaddressed and unresolved frequently fester, impacting performance and making you look bad.

Five-Star Bosses demonstrate high EI, giving them the stamina and skills to understand what is going on inside of themselves and avoid overreacting to their emotions. They sense what others are feeling and are able to respond in such a way that others improve their emotions and respond in a positive manner. It's the equivalent of having a healthy parent in charge of the family.

Five-Star Boss Questions:

1. What was an aha you got from this chapter?
2. Describe a person you've interacted with who seemed to have low EI. What were the characteristics?
3. Think of someone you've known with high EI. How did this person respond to a difficult person or situation?
4. Name one or two examples of when you may have responded to a situation with low EI.
5. When have you responded with high EI?

Chapter 19

Boss as Coach

Basic Skills to Develop Your People

Director or Developer

Most bosses are under the assumption they're company traffic cops, telling people where to go, blowing the whistle, gesturing who should stop and who should proceed, and controlling workflow in busy intersections. But Five-Star Bosses see themselves more like Yoda, the scratchy-voiced sage from *Star Wars*; they focus on developing those around them to handle their responsibilities well. So while your managerial colleagues are probably handing out directives to their team members, I challenge you to think differently.

Manager-as-Coach is about developing people more than projects and reports. As a result, your team gets stronger, making your job easier. But it's not that way at the start; you have other work to do, you have deadlines to meet, and you have some people who may lean toward lazy and prefer to be told what to do rather than think on their own. So while you were hired or promoted to oversee people, the job description focused on outcomes versus processes. But if you switch the process to growing your team, you'll be able to produce superior outcomes.

Socrates was a Greek philosopher who lived in the 400s BC. He popularized a unique teaching method whereby people uncover truth through dialogue, far less lecture-oriented than most classrooms model. The idea is to discover new things by asking strategic questions that reveal illogical conclusions, to be replaced by logical ones. The power of Socratic method for managerial coaching offers these unique aspects:

- Both teacher and student are actively engaged in dialogue.
- The process teaches the student to think, elevating confidence and competence.
- The student is more likely to own the decision.

Obviously this is a simplified version we're introducing here, but it is the essence of modern executive coaching, where a trained coach assists a leader in coming up with answers. The coach may have little knowledge of what the leader does, but the process catalyzes new thoughts and practices within the leader. The challenge of this method is that it initially takes more time and can frustrate team members who'd rather be told what to do, so they don't have to think. Yet, as you can imagine, the better the employee gets at thinking for herself, the more proficient she'll become, requiring far less of your time trouble-shooting issues. You'll be interrupted less because team members are making decisions on their own. Although the idea in theory is to work yourself out of a job, Five-Star Bosses never do because so few others develop their people at work.

Boss As Coach Style

Cop (Director)	Coach (Developer)
Answer-Giver: "Here's what you need to do."	Question-Asker: "What do you think we need to do?"
Problem Solver: Bring your problems to me and I'll give you an answer.	Tie Breaker: Bring your problems along with 2-3 solutions; I'll help you select the best one.
Adds value to the company by offering good results.	Multiplies value by developing people who can think and decide.

From Zone to Man-to-Man

In various team sports, a player can either defend via zone (this is your area, protect it) or man-to-man (stick to a person wherever he or she goes). The organizational equivalent is to work with your team as a whole or begin focusing more individualized attention. The latter is more time-consuming at first but produces the highest yield long-term.

Most teams have weekly meetings. Although you can implement coaching strategies in your team meetings, it's more productive during one-on-one interactions. That means if you're not currently doing this, you'll need to begin. The idea is taking your role as a critical thinker and decision-maker and instilling that in your people. Here's a simple example comparing a typical manager with one using a coaching method.

Team Member (TM): "I just found out that corporate is late getting us the numbers we need to create our plan for tomorrow's meeting."

Boss: "Okay, bummer. Let me contact them and see if I can get them to get it to us this afternoon. If they do, I'll immediately pass them on to you but if not, we'll need to postpone our plan or maybe even the whole meeting, since that was the main thing we needed to do."

TM: "Okay, let me know what you find out."

Boss: "I will."

A boss-as-coach conversation might go something like this:

TM: "I just found out that corporate is late getting us the numbers we need to create our plan for tomorrow's meeting."

Boss: "Okay, what do you propose that we do?"

TM: "Well, I suppose you could call HQ and see if you can speed up the process so we could get it today."

Boss: "Okay, what else would make sense?"

TM: "Maybe we just postpone our plan or the meeting until we get the stats. Otherwise, it wouldn't make sense for us to invest the time."

Boss: "That makes sense. Anything else?"

TM: "Well, I don't know how much power he has, but I could talk to my counterpart at HQ, since his boss is the woman who is in charge of the data. Perhaps he could move things along faster."

Boss: "Okay, so of these three possibilities, which do you think makes the most sense?"

TM: "I guess it might come down to either you or me using our contacts at HQ, to see if we can rattle their cage a bit. Your connection is probably stronger, since you're the boss."

Boss: "What's the downside of that?"

TM: "Wow, I'm not sure, but perhaps if you've been asking a lot from them lately, it would just be one more thing that might use up your asks. What do you think?"

Boss: "I think that's a good point. The first thing that came to mind was I could call them, but you're right, I have a big ask next month when it comes to funding salary raises, so what if we tried your contact and then let me know right away how confident he is that he can make it happen. Then if you let me know it won't, I'll make the call."

TM: "Okay, that makes sense. I'll do it."

Boss: "Cool, good job coming up with ideas. Let me know this afternoon whatever happens."

This is a simple example of the kinds of interactions that take place every day. Obviously, the coaching one took more time, but it also empowered the team member in addition to coming up with an alternative that wasn't considered prior. Plus, it potentially took one more thing off your to-do list. It also affirmed your staff member for working his network to make things happen.

Core Questions

Here are five go-to questions you can use in a variety of situations. Naturally, you'll need to adapt them to the context. Chances are you can use these as the starter or default set. After a while, your team members will already think of these before coming to you with a problem.

- What are the conditions surrounding this situation?
- What are two or three ways to solve this problem?
- What would be the risks and benefits of each of these?
- What do you think we should do and why?
- What might we be missing here?

If possible, avoid questions that can be answered with binary responses, such as "yes" or "no." The reason is that you want to engage second-level thinking. If you do this, tag on a secondary question pertaining to why you think this or how you can resolve it. For example, instead of asking, "Do you think we can improve our performance next time?" you can ask "How can we improve our performance next time?" or "What would improve our performance next time?" Single-response questions, outside of mathematics, rarely challenge team members sufficiently to develop their own managerial solutions.

As you can see, the above questions are similar to the chapter on critical thinking, but here we're applying them to developing your team members. Every week offers an array of situations where your members can hone their skills and get better. The big issue is that most bosses take shortcuts in telling employees what to do and as a result, people don't grow significantly. Variations of these questions might work better in your situation. Come up with your own list and then consider laminating these for your other team leaders or even your individual members, so that they come to you with more solutions than problems. In addition to the go-to short list, go deeper and develop a repertoire of 20-30 go-to options. This avoids redundancy.

> Sometimes Management is about making the hard decisions or having the tough conversations about performance, or people not getting along. Other times, it's being in the role of a facilitator. My wife often tells me that she just wants to be heard; she doesn't necessarily need to have me solve her problem. Too often when I became a new manager, I just want to fix everything and be done with it. But that doesn't teach my staff how to solve their own problems, nor does it help my supervisors empower their employees to work out issues. -John Otoshi

Jeopardy Method

The popular game show Jeopardy employs a technique you'll want to use. The host provides answers that contestants respond to with appropriate questions. Many bosses shun asking questions because they feel the responsibility of having the answers. "It's why they pay me the big bucks." But the Jeopardy method recognizes that knowing the best answer enables you to ask the most productive questions. It's the method we teach adults to use when coaching young leaders in our KidLead curricula. A coach observes a young leader and whispers questions applicable for the moment. For example, if a leader is not holding his team to the task and time is running out, a parent or teacher might say, "Hurry, you only have three minutes left." That's handing the leader the answer on a silver tray. Instead, when he or she realizes time is running low, the coach leans in and whispers, "Are you aware of the time?" or "What could you do to get your team to finish on time?" Questions like these elevate awareness on key issues without stating the answer. The goal is to develop leader thinking, not just complete the project.

The manager-as-coach allows you to lead people who are more intelligent or experienced than you by tapping their ability and potential. Studies show that although leaders may have above-average IQ, they often aren't the most intelligent people in the room. That's okay, because the role of the leader is to bring out the best in people and help the team function in unity. One of the most challenging things you'll face as a new manager is to convey humility, admitting that you don't always know the best answers. Getting to the better solution often takes Socratic coaching. Like all skill development, this takes time and practice. A lot of coaching skill resources are available. You can even get certified as a coach, whether or not you have an academic degree.

Five-Star Bosses know that coaching team members via asking strategic questions is one of the most productive ways to develop team members. It's also highly motivational and progressively reduces the manager's workload. The risk is that initially it requires more time and may be rejected by lazy thinkers. Cognitive misers abound, people who'd rather be told what to do than figure it out themselves. Five-Star Bosses understand that sometimes you need to call the shot yourself and make directives when time is of the essence or in emergency situations. But these tend to be limited to unique situations. When doctors are training residents, they rely heavily on the Socratic method, so don't think it won't work in situations like yours.

Five-Star Boss Questions:

1. What was an aha you got from this chapter?
2. Why do you think so few bosses use the manager-as-coach method?
3. Come up with a situation and explain a traditional boss response (directive) along with a coaching approach (developmental), similar to the example described in this chapter.
4. What will you need to do differently to begin employing this method?
5. Think of a specific situation you need to address in the next week, and rehearse in your mind a coach approach with a team member.

Chapter 20
Tapping Into Power

Finding Influence in Interesting Places

Defining Power

My wife is the executive director of an upscale senior living facility in Calabasas, a small city teaming with media celebrities and corporate leaders. During the recent fires in that area, they evacuated their residents to sister facilities in Encino and Hollywood. It's a good thing they did, because the fires came within half a mile of their building. Electricity poles burned, causing a power outage. So even those powerful people living in Calabasas and Malibu couldn't control the power of Mother Nature.

Everyone understands the importance of power, but none more than those who lack it. One thing I've learned over the course of 60 years is that the person who wins isn't the one who is right, but rather who has the most power. Many bosses feel frustrated that they don't have more power. They complain about being unable to change things, to make things happen. Listen to most groups of managers and you'll hear victim talk, such as "I told my supervisor, but she didn't listen…," "You just can't change things around this place," and "If you're not the lead dog, the view never changes." No one enjoys feeling powerless. What most new and ineffective bosses fail to understand is the many ways they can obtain power, beyond their positions.

We'll define power as *the potential to influence people to do things that you want*. If this sounds potentially sinister, it is. Power, in the hands of an unethical and/or incompetent person, has the potential to hurt people and corrupt an organization. History is full of examples of this. You've probably witnessed this yourself. Yet because of this, power needs to be understood and embraced by those who would use it for good. Avoiding power because of its potential for evil is naïve and futile. A powerless leader is an oxymoron. You can't lead without it. Only when good people learn to gain and use power effectively can we hope to thwart the efforts of self-centered and maniacal influencers.

Power Sources

Here are seven sources that will keep the lights on in your managing, even when it seems like your position is in a power outage. These also explain how people get things done beyond their "pay grade."

1. *Coercion/Fear*: Although this is not a source you'll want to invest in if you want to be an effective manager, you need to realize that it exists and that people who are generally self-centered and/or desperate resort to this. The neighborhood bully is visible in corporate and national leaders, winning by intimidation and "persuading" people through fear and punishment. While we don't advocate this, we need to

acknowledge its short-term ability to change the behaviors of others. You may need to tap this source if a person you're facing is using it. Throughout history, entire cultures have been liberated and kept free by the willingness to go up against bullies using weapons of war.

2. *Legitimate/Positional*: A majority assumes this is the main or sole source of power within an organization. Granted, most positions include a certain amount of power. As a result, some spend huge sums of money and effort to obtain certain positions because of the power resources inherent in a role (i.e. President of the United States). Yet we all know people who fill positions and fail to use their power well, along with those who misuse and abuse it. Bossy managers rely on positional power solely, while some managers transcend legitimate power. That's because they add one or more of the following power sources to it, compounding their influence.

3. *Relationships/Social*: Another term for this source of power is *referent*. Think of it in terms of to whom you can refer, who you know, who they know, and who knows you. (Make sure you read the chapter on Social Banking.) Although the "old boy network" is typically thought of negatively, it's little more than an example of a network of allies. This comes in discovering similarities and spending time together on the golf course, tennis court, or in backyard barbeques. Research indicates that men are typically stronger at this than women. Therefore, women need to be more intentional in investing time with people who possess influence. This may be colleagues, supervisors, and those who can open doors and add value to what you do. Who you know is often more important than what you know. Who you can contact to help solve problems can be as valuable as being able to fix things yourself.

One of the great values of being a part of USC isn't just the education; it's the strong culture. Students are groomed to believe that being in the Trojan family is a lifelong benefit, in that complete strangers say "Fight on!" as they pass each other on the street whenever wearing a USC shirt or cap. One such experience I had was on the Great Wall of China, when a Chinese student sporting an SC cap made the "Fight on" gesture upon noticing my USC t-shirt. A lively, friendly conversation ensued. Online networks such as LinkedIn are also valuable, illustrating that it's not just who you know that matters but also who they know within their network. Managers should invest weekly if not daily time cultivating connections, because we're most apt to trust those we know. "Office politics" is the term people use when they're on the outside of organizational relationships. When you're on the inside, you call it "productivity."

> **Power & Influence**
>
> *Nearly all men can stand adversity, but if you want to test a man's character, give him power.* — Abraham Lincoln
>
> *The measure of a man is what he does with power.* — Plato
>
> *Knowledge is power. Power to do evil...or power to do good. Power itself is not evil. So knowledge itself is not evil.* — Veronica Roth
>
> *I met an old lady once, almost a hundred years old, and she told me, 'There are only two questions that human beings have ever fought over, all through history. How much do you love me? And Who's in charge?'* — Elizabeth Gilbert
>
> *Recognizing power in another does not diminish your own.* — Joss Whedon
>
> *Being powerful is like being a lady. If you have to tell people you are, you aren't.* — Margaret Thatcher

4. *Reward/Resources*: This power source involves available assets. What can you do to reward those who can help you? Money is an obvious example, but there are many others as well. Physical assets such as real estate, possessions, stocks, weapons, and technology are all examples of resources. The last several years, I've been a Lecturer of Management at the Naval Postgraduate School. In a typical year, over 25% of the U.S. national budget is spent on the military. One of the best ways to keep world peace is to maintain military strength. That's a resource. Muscle and

conditioning are personal strengths, which is why armed forces and para-military organizations such as police and firefighters require their staff to stay in shape. Naturally, the types of rewards and resources that add value are based on the context of the organization. Aligning with people possessing these resources (referent) is also a way to raise your value.

5. *Expertise/Talent*: Your ability to accomplish tasks better than others is typically a combination of skills (learned), expertise (familiarity), and talent (aptitude). Understanding how to code a new software program, having familiarity with social media, and being able to run or throw a baseball faster than others are examples of how expertise and talent can give you influence. Naturally, this varies from situation to situation. It explains why some entrepreneurs, while notoriously autocratic and negative in their relationships, can wield so much power in a company. Talent trumps people skills in certain situations. What can you do better than others? How can you leverage your expertise and talent to help you gain more power?

6. *Info/Knowledge*: Higher education is based on this source of power, such that people with superior understanding and thinking skills possess influence deemed important to others. When you have access to information that others do not, when you possess an understanding of how things work, and wherever you can bring added value based on your education, these are power sources. The goal is to leverage them as much as possible to make you more effective as a manager. You may want to consider a degree or certification that not only looks good on your resume but also gives you insights that others value. Naturally, insider info can be used as blackmail, but any of these power sources can result in both positive and negative outcomes. Electricity can electrocute and save lives.

7. *Personality/Charisma*: One last power source is your own personality. Although qualities like charisma tend to be more genetic and hereditary in nature, there are things you can do to

enhance your ability to speak up, cast a friendly disposition, and be likeable. Extroversion is a strong benefit for those in managerial roles. You want to get people to like you. Being positive, pleasant, and amenable are characteristics of leveraging your personality for your benefit. Naturally, this aligns well with the relational/social power source. In fact, most of these sources intermix with each other. But at the end of the day, your personality has a lot to do in terms of shaping how people perceive you and thus how they'll respond to you as a manager.

Summary: The good news of this chapter is that regardless of the level of your role within your organization, you can become a more significant influencer by tapping multiple power sources. This is not manipulation, unless you're using it for selfish purposes. If you're employing them to advance the organization and serve your colleagues and team members, you'll be perceived as a Five-Star Boss. Remember, a powerless leader is ineffective. How you obtain power and then how you use it will determine whether or not you're going to make a positive difference in the role you occupy.

Five-Star Boss Questions:

1. On a sheet of paper, write numbers 1 through 7 in the left margin. Write examples of each of the seven power sources that make sense in the context of your organization. These can be constructive and destructive.
2. Circle or list three or four ways that you can increase your power in your current role (thinking beyond position/title).
3. List two or three people of influence in your organization who can offer advice on gaining influence. How will you connect with them within the next month?
4. When did you experience a power-outage in terms of trying to get something accepted at work that was denied?
5. Looking back, what could you have done to increase your influence in this situation?

Chapter 21
Badass Meetings
How to Rock Your Gatherings

Love or Loathe?

Bad news: As of this book's publication, the average U.S. employee invests more than five hours per week in meetings that require four hours of out-of-meeting preparation. Managers average over 12 hours of meetings a week (14 hours for the public sector). The average employee attends more than 60 meetings per month, over a third of which are deemed a waste of time. Unnecessary meetings are now considered the #1 time-waster at work. It's estimated that unnecessary meetings cost U.S. companies $37 billion annually. And consistently near or at the top of lists describing what people don't like about work is meetings.

Good news: If you want to be considered a rock star in your role as the boss, do what you can to design meetings that are productive, enjoyable, and efficient. Your challenge is straddling the tension between efficiency and productivity. Therefore, it's important for you to create a culture of great meetings. Your people will bless you, and your reputation will spread throughout your organization. Following are Five-Star Boss practices for running badass meetings.

Why: Make sure you consider why a meeting is needed. If it involves a brainstorming session, a monthly report, or a weekly check-in, then name it at the top of the agenda. A declarative statement provides a sense of purpose and justification to people being there. If the meeting is for reporting, perhaps an email would suffice. Challenge the logic of meetings you're in charge of so that you don't just meet to meet or because you've always done it that way. Declaring a clear "why" establishes a value along with expectations.

Who: Who needs to be in the meeting? Why does each person need to be there? Is there a specific time in the agenda that's applicable? For example, Sarah is in charge of the sales report, providing an update for your team quarterly revenues for your division. Instead of including her in the weekly 1-hour 8 a.m. meeting, schedule her for 8:15-8:30, allowing her to invest 15-20 minutes instead of 60. If you want the entire team to have a sense of what everyone is doing, then let them know that in advance and structure reporting for specific content, metrics, and goals. If possible, limit strategic meetings to four to seven people. After seven attendees, productivity goes down and passivity rises. Team dynamics affect meetings, so consider this when inviting people.

Prep Issues: What do you need to cover? The danger is assuming that everyone knows what's going to happen. Create an agenda and send it to people at least 24 hours prior to the meeting; more, if prep work is needed. This creates a warm environment for discussion. It also relaxes people, giving the perception that you've worked at making the meeting productive. An exception is if an item is controversial, as you don't want to create a negatively charged attitude going into the meeting. Agenda items can be allotted time and tagged as one of three expectations: "I" for information only, "C" for conversation, and "D" for decision. Again, this establishes expectations coming into the meeting and also provides participants with a sense of preparation.

Community Building: Team meetings offer effective ways to bond as a team. A quick check-in, where each member shares a high and low in his/her life, provides an opportunity to feel more like a family than a sterile work group. This is especially important if you have Affiliators, people motivated by relationships. If you jump into the agenda without a warm greeting and rapport building, these members will be less effective during the meeting. This technique also enhances cohesion, if that is a need. If neither of these are relevant to your team, then you'll want to minimize this feature. If your supervisor is in the meeting, you'll want to defer to his/her personal preference. Power and Achievement people will see community building as a waste of time. An Affiliation-oriented boss will applaud the more relational approach. (See chapters on motivation.)

Time Issues: When should you meet? Experts who study attitude fluctuations on weekly and daily schedules note that people are generally the most positive between 10 a.m. and 3 p.m., Tuesday through Friday. Thus, you may want to avoid Monday meetings altogether and earlier morning and later afternoon times, if possible. How long do you allot for each item? Is this realistic? A schedule is like a budget, because time is literally money in a business meeting. If the average salary is $80K per person, a 2-hour meeting of 10 people would cost the company $770. Is this good ROI (return on investment)? Could it be more productive in half the time or with half the people present? If you notice a tendency to run long, keep a clock in front of your line of sight or consider assigning a time monitor who signals you.

Norms: Convey meeting expectations early as the boss. You're establishing a micro-culture for your team. For example, is it okay to show up 5-15 minutes late, or is punctuality a demand? When my wife worked for John Maxwell, timeliness was valued, so that at 8 a.m. the door was closed and you were not to enter after it was shut. That created a pretty strong culture on punctuality, with minimal tardiness. Is it a no-screen zone, so that cellphones are face-down on the table? Are food and drinks welcome? Is there a fixed seating arrangement, or is there a formal or informal assignment? You're the boss, so if you called the meeting, establish protocol. Push back when people ignore the norms; be kind yet firm.

Process: Is the meeting primarily strategic or tactical? If the meeting has multiple items on the agenda, you may want to identify the approach for each. Here's the reason: tactical issues tend to take more time and are usually fulfilled by people lower on the totem pole. Leaders typically focus more on strategic matters, delegating the details to others. Therefore, it's important for you to determine which approach to take. The temptation is for people to get stuck in the weeds, deliberating numerous specifics that could be done with fewer people in a different meeting. A common mistake of less experienced leaders is trying to control too much, instead of delegating tactical issues to a team who then reports back for information and for approval, as needed. (See next two graphs for examples.)

Strategic	Tactical
We need an internal marketing campaign, to make sure everyone understands the new policy.	Why don't we set up info tables at the main entrance and in the breakroom? We could incentivize them to sign up by…
Let's partner with a couple of local charities. This will kick off the CSR program and cast the vision.	Let's brainstorm some non-profits that we can think of and then we'll go back to the list and consider issues we can get behind to determine our partners.
We'll meet with administration to make sure they approve of our project.	Josh and I will set up a meeting with the VP and then include a written brief for the board. I think we can do the 2nd Monday…

Tips for Running Great Meetings

1. Know Where You've Been: Unless the agenda is brand-new, provide a brief overview of where you've been, what's been decided, and who's to have done what. That means you'll want to do your homework—know in advance what should be shared in terms of previous meeting notes and accomplishments. People are busy, and they'll benefit from knowing what has been done so far, so you don't waste time on things that have already been discussed.

2. State the Goal: When you're leading a meeting, your success to a certain degree is based on accomplishing a goal. What is the goal of this meeting, and how does it fit in the big picture of your organization? Don't assume other people know the goal. By declaring the goal and even writing it for people to see, you help everyone be responsible for sticking to the issue. Plus, you can tell if you were effective or not at the end. Obviously, you may need to do some prep work in advance so you'll know what to say and how you'll accomplish your goal.

3. Pace Discussion: Ever attend a boring meeting? We all have. Good leaders know how to pace a meeting so there's enough tension to make it interesting, but not so rushed that people feel they've not been able to participate. This is a difficult skill to develop. Help talkers get to their point; know when it's time to change subjects and end a discussion or engage people who've become bored or started talking to each other instead of the entire group. Five-Star Bosses pace meetings well.

4. Keep the Focus: Meetings can be interesting while having little to do with the goal of a meeting. Your job, as meeting leader, is to help your team stay focused on the goal. A good question to ask yourself when someone is talking is, "What does this have to do with our goal?" If your answer is "I don't know," then you may want to ask the speaker, "Justin, help me understand what this has to do with the objective of our meeting." Some rabbit trails are helpful. Most are not. You'll be judged on your ability to discern these well.

5. Manage Personalities: Every team has different temperaments along with various experiences, intelligence, and emotions. What you want to do as a leader is help everyone work together to accomplish the goal of the meeting. This may require you to manage a conflict, help people who feel confident in talking to listen more, and encourage quieter people to express their ideas. Doing this in a caring, honoring way is not easy. Stay positive. Smile. Make eye contact. Use the names of people to make them feel honored. Scan the room for body language that indicates people are disengaged or feel alienated.

6. Seek Broad Input: Everyone doesn't need to share equally, but everyone should speak. You want to make sure that some individuals do not dominate the meeting and others remain silent. There are nice ways of asking people who've talked a lot to listen and encouraging ways for quiet people to share their ideas. "John, what do you think about this?" "Let's have some of you who've not shared yet tell us what you're thinking." In difficult situations, you can even resort to using a "talking stick," a physical item that must be in the person's possession before they can speak. Using this even a few times teaches members to be more conversational and less lecturing.

7. Consider Mini-Meetings & Sub-Teams: One way to gain a lot of ideas quickly and help people feel like they've participated is to break up into groups of 2-4, assigning them 1-3 minutes for brainstorming, discussion, or strategizing. By doing this, you maximize your time instead of having one person talking at any one time. Plus, quieter people feel more comfortable sharing their thoughts with 1-3 others than in groups of 6-12. You can assign different tasks for each sub-team or let them all work on the same issue. Then let each team report on what it discussed.

8. Stand or Sit? Sometimes it's good to stand when you're leading a meeting, and sometimes it's better to sit. Sitting creates more of a feel that we're all on the same level, and if there are eight or fewer people in a small room, standing may seem awkward, as people stare at your torso instead of your face. Standing is good if the room is large, you're writing on a whiteboard or flip chart, and if you need a bit more authority for whatever reason. It says "I'm in charge" more than if you're sitting. My wife's daily "standing meeting" at her work was turning into a 60- to 75-minute sit-down meeting, so when everyone literally stood, they cut it down to 20-30 minutes.

9. Write or Not Write? When you're the meeting leader, sometimes you'll want to write ideas on a flip chart or whiteboard. The benefit is that your team can see what is being discussed and your scribe can record what is posted. The question is whether you should do it yourself or select someone else. If it is a potentially controversial subject, you may want to do the writing yourself so you can select the terms you prefer, reduce wording that is emotion-laden, and even order them in a way that you want as a leader, thus retaining more control. The benefit of asking someone else to write is that you can keep your eyes on the team and not turn your back on them while they wait for you to write, and if your writing isn't clear, you can select someone whose is.

10. Review & Record: Before the meeting ends, you'll want to be sure that your scribe has a sense of what should be recorded. You can provide your own overview of what was accomplished, or you may want to ask your scribe to do that. Be sure you end your regular meeting in time for you to provide a 1- to 2-minute overview of what was accomplished and, if possible, talk about HOW the team functioned. Then thank them. Depending on the content, you may want to have someone email a brief overview of the meeting, listing decisions made and assignments clarified. This gives absentees a summary and holds participants accountable. It's also a reference if someone forgets what he or she was to do.

Continual Improvement

You can establish your own list of meeting commandments. Then after every meeting or perhaps every month or two, provide a meeting analysis. This could be something as simple as you and another person going over each point and assessing how it went. It could also involve everyone's participation, using the list as a guideline. In higher education, we use rubrics, a quality expectation table that lists three to six different themes and then provides characteristics of each based on "opportunity to improve," "good," "met expectations" and "exceeded expectations." You can do a similar thing by grading each agenda item on a 1-4 Likert scale, such as 1-room for growth, 2-fair, 3-good, 4-excellent. Then you can average each and make sure that if the average goes below a 3.0, you invest more time and energy into designing the meetings and managing them, until you are consistently over 3.0. Average bosses move into status quo for their meetings, whereas Five-Star Bosses continually monitor the quality of their gatherings, striving to keep them high-caliber.

There are a number of great books with advice on running effective meetings. The irony is that few people who lead meetings have ever studied effective meeting management. You can establish a new day in your company by being more intentional about who, what, when, and how you conduct your gatherings. People will appreciate your respect for their time and chances are, you'll be nominated to facilitate other meetings, since it's such a common challenge in organizations today.

Misc. Ideas

- Consider keeping a log of best and worst practices in meetings you've observed, as a way to remember what to do and not do in meetings you facilitate. This also becomes a great training resource as you develop your team members.
- Parkinson's Law states that work expands to fill the amount of time allotted to it. While you don't want to rush agenda items, generally they'll take as much time as you make for them, so make sure not to budget too much time.
- Opinions vary in terms of how you set an agenda. The order of items can affect the results. Some suggest you should put the more difficult items early on the agenda, when energy is higher, to avoid meeting fatigue. Another idea is to place potentially controversial decisions toward the end, when people will tend to pass them just to get done. Although it sounds a bit manipulative, if you have an adversary in the meeting who must

- arrive late or leave early, consider scheduling that item when she or he is gone.
- Offer other people an opportunity to facilitate a regular team meeting. This is great for Power-oriented people (see chapters on motivation), plus it lets you see who may be skilled in this area, along with helping people understand how difficult it is.
- During planning sessions, consider designating an official Devil's Advocate whose responsibility is to challenge ideas. Select a new person each meeting so no one becomes known as a naysayer and forms a reputation or negative self-image.
- Consider different locations for a change of pace, since the surroundings can impact the feel of a meeting. You'll naturally want to avoid distractions, but meeting outdoors, in a coffee shop, or at a café can help. When I lived near Silicon Valley, I'd often see Apple employees meeting in Starbucks—relaxed but very focused on their agendas.
- Be careful who you assign the note taking, as this is a potentially influential role in terms of how things are worded and recorded for reference. Select a person who is positive and thorough, yet supportive of you (along with having good writing skills).

Five-Star Boss Questions:

1. What were the top two or three ideas you gleaned from this chapter?
2. What best practices have you seen that you'd have added to this chapter?
3. What are the two or three things you want to do better in your meetings?
4. What are the two or three things you want to stop doing in your meetings?
5. If you have an upcoming meeting to facilitate, create an agenda with intended outcomes and a timeline.

Chapter 22
Bodacious Brainstorming

Effective Ideation

To Solve Problems, Storm Them

Five-Star Bosses are in the problem-solving business, regardless of their industry. Although they enjoy everything going well, that's not why their organization pays and empowers them. But their responsibility is not to figure out and solve what's wrong on their own. As the boss, they're responsible for bringing the best solutions to light, which is why they do this as part of a team. Whether the problem is to increase sales, improve product quality, or resolve some other unmet need, they frequently need to storm problems.

The term "brainstorm sessions" was coined by an advertising expert named Osborn in the early 1940s, as he tried to get his staff to think more creatively. The idea was to storm a problem in order to come up with more effective solutions. Osborn wrote about the process in a couple of books that became bestsellers. The four rules for effective brainstorming are:

1. Strive for quantity over quality.
2. Withhold criticism; suspend judgement.
3. Welcome wild and crazy ideas.
4. Combine and improve ideas.

As a boss, you'll need to periodically facilitate brainstorm sessions—meetings designed to come up with innovative and unique ideas to solve problems, take products or services to the next level, and help your organization thrive. Companies and groups within them vary as to their level of innovation. Some are more open to new ideas, while others are staid and stable. Naturally, we'd think a marketing team is more creative than an accounting department. My point is that your role as the boss will be easier or more difficult depending on the individuals invited to this session. This chapter offers some of the best practices for getting the most out of brainstorming.

Over the last several years, my work with young leaders has revealed a strong tendency for people to jump on a good idea early instead of developing an array of ideas and then selecting the greatest one. The enemy of great is good. Don't just consider brainstorming an annual event that you do during an offsite retreat. Brainstorm frequently, in short bursts. The key is how you facilitate the process. Following Osborn's four rules well is not easy, because people get lazy and distracted and certain personalities have a more difficult time being open to new ideas than others. But like any new skill, with a little exercise you can train your team to do fast brainstorms to address any number of issues that come your way.

The first three rules will likely require you to be actively involved in creating and controlling a safe environment so that everyone feels comfortable sharing ideas, regardless of how outlandish or crazy they may sound. Chances are you'll need to establish ground rules each time as a friendly reminder of conditions for great brainstorming. For example, suspending judgement isn't just about saying an idea isn't good; it also means not labeling an idea as good. When you or others give some ideas a thumbs-up or say "that's good" or "I like that," you're often shutting down the process. The reason is that people begin feeling a pressure to perform, to come up with other good or even better suggestions. Even though it's well meaning, it's counterproductive.

Especially avoid labeling ideas as the boss, because people will want to impress you and your approval might limit ideas quite different from the ones you deem good. Instead, declare the goal for coming up with—drumroll, please—50 ideas. Select the goal randomly if you like, but make it large enough to be quantity-oriented and not allow time to critique or get lost on rabbit trails. If time is limited, set a 15- to 45-minute window during which no one comments or shares an opinion about any ideas, verbally and nonverbally. Obviously some ideas will need explanation, but again, this is not the time to critique, only clarify.

Brainstorming

Strive for quantity over quality
(the best ideas are rarely the first ones; they evolve; establish quotas that challenge you)

Withhold criticism; suspend judgement
(there are no bad ideas; there also are no good ones in this phase; avoid any kind of qualitative labeling)

Welcome wild and crazy ideas
("stupid" and "unrealistic" ideas often break invisible seals preventing really great ones from emerging; laud the ludicrous)

Combine and improve ideas
(sometimes opposites attract, meaning you never know how mating ideas can result in amazing offspring)

SIB: The Creativity Cycle

Research findings push back on two common myths about creativity. One is that creativity is spontaneous, and the other is that either you're creative or you're not. Let's address the spontaneous myth first. The best ideas are rarely generated out of the blue, in midair. Rather, they're usually the result of study followed by an incubation period when your subconscious is processing the information. Then the birthing process results in any number of new and diverse possibilities.

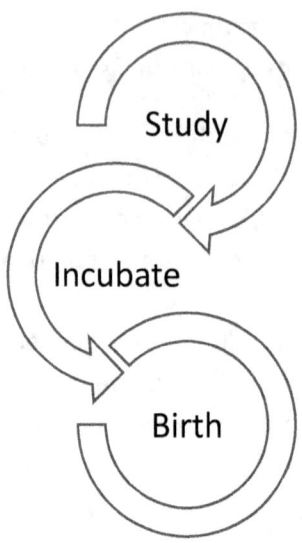

Study: The more you know about a subject, the more likely you are to come up with effective ideas related to the issue. Reading, experimenting, talking to experts, and concentrated discussions are ways to think more deeply about what it is you're striving to solve. In the context of a typical work project, consider assigning "research" tasks to team members prior the meeting.

Incubate: If the study stage is the equivalent of putting a bunch of art materials on a table for a child, the incubate stage is telling the child to go have fun with them. The benefit of filling the conscious mind with ideas and information related to the problem is that your subconscious can then process these. This "child" will have fun playing with the materials even when you're unaware of it. This even happens during sleep. Great inventors awaken with breakthrough ideas because their brains kept working during the night and were less distracted.

Birth: Giving birth to new ideas is a much more natural process if you've provided a sufficient gestation period of research followed by incubation. If you're working on a big project, you may want to use the SIB cycle two to three times, allowing each rotation to process the ideas at higher and higher levels. Make sure to record these ideas so you don't lose ground between sessions.

Managing Naysayers

The old saying goes, "Every party needs a party pooper. That's why we invited you." Just because you're the boss doesn't mean you can control everyone's response to ideas that don't seem plausible. Chances are you'll have team members with personalities that have a more difficult time suspending judgement. "C'mon, man, we don't have the budget or manpower to implement that idea." "You've got to be kidding. Where are you living, Mars?" "We already tried that." These and any number of related gestures, such as rolling the eyes, leaning back with crossed arms, frowning, and clenching the jaw, all telegraph a negative judgment.

So how do you respond to a Negative Ned? Well, if you know Ned is going to be in the meeting, you may want to pull him (or her) aside prior to the meeting and offer some coaching. Don't assume that Ned has ever been trained on practices of creativity or brainstorming. Politely and respectfully remind Ned that since others in the room respect his opinion, it's important for him to remain positive in today's meeting and if that's not possible, to at least be neutral. Remind him that the goal of the session is NOT to refine the best solution, but rather to come up with a good number of ideas, and from these do triage to determine the best ones. Creating this sense of accountability is all that most people will need. If Ned does well or does not do well, follow up with some feedback. If it's an affirmation, then offer a thumbs-up or Starbucks gift card or "nice job!" If it's not good, then arrange a short meeting as soon as possible to offer clear and specific feedback. Most of the time,

Negative Neds aren't intentionally being critical; it's just how they're wired, so they need feedback to recalibrate their communication.

Whenever possible, avoid inviting Negative Neds to brainstorming sessions. The reason is that people like him are typically stronger when it comes to refining an idea than developing new ones. You can affirm him later in the process by including him. If you can't avoid his participation, then clearly establish the creativity best practices and post them for everyone to see, whether it's on a media slide, whiteboard, or flip chart page. If you sense members are neglecting these, then push the pause button for a time-out to revisit the brainstorming guidelines. After a while team members get it, because this is part of the norming stage of development.

Let me comment on one more thing regarding the influence of personalities in a brainstorming session. Often an idea is judged based on who births it. For example, if I said, "Abraham Lincoln wrote that power should be in the hands of the people," we'd like that statement more than if I said, "Adolf Hitler wrote that power should be in the hands of the people." Sometimes the perceived value of an idea is skewed by the person who brings it, based on if she is less popular or is pushy or even if she's charismatic or has a high IQ. One way to level the playing field for all ideas is to have everyone write their ideas on Post-It notes and then stick them to a wall. You can ask people before the meeting to bring 5-10 ideas, one per note, or do this at the start of the meeting. It's a way to detach an idea from its source so that you weigh it on its merits and not on the reputation of the person who birthed it.

Lessons From the #1 Creative Co.

Many refer to IDEO, located in the Silicon Valley, as the most creative organization in the world. We use products every day that they helped designed. They're primarily known for engineering solutions on how items are used and dispensed. For example, the upside-down ketchup, mustard, and toothpaste containers are the results of this firm's work. They helped design the first Apple computer mouse, dental floss dispensers, and countless other high- and low-tech items. An interesting thing is that their solution teams usually consist of people with diverse backgrounds, not just engineers. Members may include a psychologist, educator, medical student, marketer, or any number of other professionals. The power of this is you get a variety of views, not just one, each of which can bring a different perspective to play. That is why it might help at times to invite non-team members to your larger brainstorming sessions, simply for variety.

Another thing IDEO does is avoid roles or positions during these meetings. Meeting facilitation is given to the person most adept at it, not the boss or owner. Everyone is on the same level. While you may have two or three people responsible to organize the process and make sure it's moving along, it's otherwise an even playing field.

If the solution is a tangible one, various test models are created and then tested, primarily with end-user feedback provided. The goal is to fail fast so that you can learn from potential fixes and then improve on them. Naturally, this may or may not fit the situation, but avoid investing too much time on a single fix when you can create multiple tests. Sometimes you don't know what you need until you try it, so failing fast and often offers a lot of feedback for coming up with the best outcome. You can find more IDEO info online, including ABC's "Deep Dive" interview. Watching this as a team could help establish a norm to storm problems more effectively.

Ideal Ideating

Here are a variety of ways to juice up the ideation process, depending on the size and scope of the problem you're striving to solve.

- *Suggestion box:* Use an ongoing suggestion box and when possible, post suggestions along with responses so people can

see that you actually read them. If you don't convey a way of acknowledging these, people will stop using them.
- *Prep materials:* Make sure you provide an array of writing and even doodling resources to record and post ideas. Part of this has to do with kinesthetic learning, meaning some of your people think better when they're drawing and moving their hands. Make sure you have adequate flip chart paper (along with ways to post them visually), fresh bold markers, and such.
- *Scribe tag team*: Take turns delegating note-taking to those who write clearly and are adept at succinctly putting ideas on paper, so as not to skew the meaning. Variety keeps people engaged.
- *Snoop trip:* Take your team to visit another company, whether or not it is in your industry. Getting an inside look at how other companies function can offer insights that you can apply to your own. This might be a 2-hour tour followed by a lunch discussion. One publishing company I worked for toured both the last remaining Kodak film processing plant and the New Belgium brewery—vastly diverse companies, but both intriguing.
- *Idea wall:* Offer an idea wall where people can write on a whiteboard and post ideas on sticky notes. Sometimes a designated space for posting ideas will stimulate more ideas. You can do this physically in a room or electronically using an online forum.
- *Changing places*: Consider getting out of the building. Sometimes the environment can stifle creativity, so think about meeting in a nearby home, hotel room, park, or retreat center. If your company has a meeting room, consider bartering with another company to swap rooms, requiring no budget but providing a new view. Don't underestimate the environment. Avoid noisy, distracting settings.
- *Pace the process.* Naturally, this has more to do with longer brainstorm sessions than mini-problem solving, but offering refreshments, short breaks each hour, and fun activities to re-engage people are effective. Good brainstorming is as draining as it is invigorating, so pacing the process is your job as a boss.

Five-Star Boss Questions:

1. Which of the ideas in this chapter did you find most interesting?
2. What ideas would you add to the chapter that you've seen be helpful?
3. What are a couple of problems you're facing that could benefit from a brainstorm session?
4. How will you train your team on brainstorming?
5. Who are the Negative Neds at your work? How will you help them not adversely affect the ideation process?

Chapter 23

Sitch Leading

Selecting the Style That Fits the Situation

Right Tool, Right Place

I'm not much of a fix-it guy, but growing up on a farm in Iowa, I spent hours at a time handing tools to my dad while he repaired tractors and machinery. I know the difference between Vise-Grips, pliers, and a socket and open- or closed-end wrenches. My dad was pretty good at looking at a bolt and identifying the size. "Hand me a 5/16 open-end," he'd say, lying under the equipment. I'd go to the toolbox, find the wrench, and hand it to him. If you've done any work like that on your own, you know you can't use a 3/8 wrench to do the work of a 5/16, or a ¼ or ½ inch for that matter. The tool needs to fit the job.

Leadership is like that. One size doesn't fit all. Maslow said, "If all you have is a hammer, everything starts looking like a nail." But in leading, the context and situation calls for a specific type of leadership. Therefore, the more tools you have in your toolbox, the more likely you'll find one that fits the situation. Two professors named Hershey and Blanchard came up with the idea on how to do this. I'll give you the skinny on the tool that we teach in our young leader training program. We call it "Sitch Leading," as it relates to selecting the right leadership style for each situation.

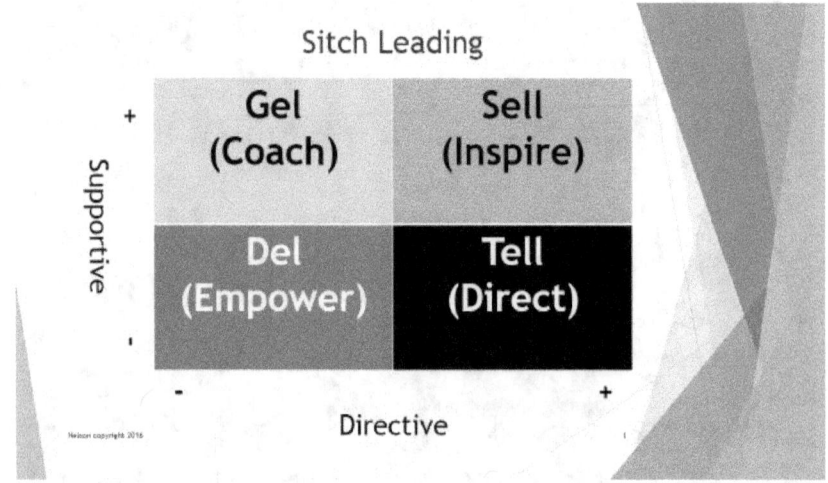

Sitch leading focuses primarily on two aspects, the motivation (commitment) of the team members and their competency (skill) for the task. A low commitment – high competence person needs something different from her leader than a high commitment – low competence person. We're all low competence in most tasks, so we're not talking about IQ or ability to learn, but rather a specific task or goal. This requires a leader to remain highly engaged, pending the conditions and the team. Let's begin in the lower right corner and work counter-clockwise around the Situational Leadership matrix.

Tell (*High Commitment – Low Competence*): In this situation, team members are highly motivated but need direction, either for coordinating as a team or in task assignments. Typically, in this case, time is of the essence. The leader needs to communicate clearly and concretely, providing a lot of input. Directive leadership is needed during an emergency, as in war conditions and para-military operations. That's why military organizations rely heavily on rank and authority, whereas normal corporate conditions would not lend themselves to this style. People would resent being told what to do and would call you "bossy" and a "drill sergeant." Yet, being able to speak up and exert authority are vital skills for bosses to possess, when conditions call for this style.

Sell (*Low Commitment – Low to Moderate Competence*): The "Sell" style involves brainstorming solutions with a team and then selling them on the one you think is best. By letting team members share ideas, you're more likely to come up with a better idea and team members feel more ownership, improving their commitment. By selling them on what you think is best, you still offer input where they lack experience or training. Then you'll need to be more involved and offer an inspirational style, to help them embrace the idea and act on it. This requires support from you, along with some education/training and on-the-job accountability.

Gel (*Moderate to High Commitment – Variable Competence*): Gelling is the process of letting liquids set up to be semi-firm. The upper left cell is when your team members possess moderate to high competence and variable commitment. A more appropriate leadership style at this point is active coaching, from a Socratic approach. Instead of telling people what to do, you're there to bring out their best. Asking strategic questions helps team members think more effectively. You assist them by directing their thinking, not telling them what to do. Because full commitment is not present, you're still involved, but you're respectful of their abilities and believe the best in them. This is also a good style when you have ample time to discuss issues and marinate on them, so that you increase buy-in and elevate understanding and ownership. Thus, you help them "gel" as a team.

Del (*High Commitment – High Competence*): The lower left cell is "Del," short for delegate. While it may not seem that you need a leader here because you have highly competent and committed team members, the leader is present to troubleshoot, monitor progress, facilitate discussions, and encourage the team. This is also known as *laissez-faire*, laid-back leading. At times you don't know who the leader is because s/he has empowered others, giving them authority to make decisions. You can't empower people unless you also give them the right to make decisions. Ultimately, the leader is responsible, so you want to make sure you trust your team members and release them to do their work.

Summary

As you can imagine, if you use the Tell method when you have highly committed and skilled team members, you'll insult them and eventually find yourself ostracized by coming on too strong. Conversely, if you're laid back when people are seeking directions, they'll perceive you as out of touch and perhaps not a leader. While these are the most obvious differences, you can set up the same comparisons for each of the four leading styles.

Most bosses possess primary and secondary preferences. Because of that, they often resort to them instead of adapting to the situation. The Five-Star Boss is able to change leadership styles according to the situation, even though this may not feel natural. People who are not adaptable tend to frustrate team members who recognize when a style is out of place. Sometimes you can see how an entire organization needs a leader who excels in a certain style. You can see this in national governments, when a leader who is considered too laid back is replaced by one who is more directive and dynamic. But when the person is unable to read the situation and respond accordingly, s/he will typically be out of a job. Organizations are dynamic, so a chameleon leader who is able to change with the environment can be more valuable than a one-shade leader.

The more tools you have in your toolbox, the more effective you can be, matching what the situation and team members need with the most effective leading style.

Five-Star Boss Questions:

1. Which of the four styles feels most natural to you?
2. What is your secondary style?
3. Which is your least comfortable?
4. Describe a situation you've experienced when the leader's style didn't match the situation.
5. Which style would have been more effective?

THE FIVE-STAR BOSS

Chapter 24
Managing Expectations
The Unwritten Law of Satisfaction

Reducing Disappointments

When our three sons were young, like most families with small kids, my wife and I had to juggle schedules. I learned quickly that if my marriage was going to remain strong, I'd need to improve my communication about my job commitments. She worked part-time and was more flexible than me, so if I had an evening meeting or out-of-town speaking engagement, I realized that I needed to convey my inability to support her with the boys, sooner rather than later. As long as I did this, her patience was amazing; but when I failed to manage expectations of parenting support, it created tension between us, justifiably so.

Today, most of my expectation management involves students. I try to offer significant information about assigned projects so they know what I expect, because no one enjoys reading a bad paper or receiving a low grade. I also manage overall grade expectations. A lot of students in the programs where I teach are competitive over-achievers who expect high grades. Unfortunately, because grade inflation is a phenomenon that most universities are striving to control, I educate students about the system's grading process that precludes that from happening. While it doesn't appease everyone, I've noticed that it significantly reduces the number of meetings I have with disgruntled students after grades are posted.

Staying Ahead of the Pain

Physicians who deal with pain recommend meds before a patient's level becomes high, because it's more difficult to knock down the pain after it's intense. This is referred to as staying ahead of the pain. While the theme of this chapter doesn't seem very proactive, the concept may be one of the most important in this book. Although "the best defense is a good offense" is often true, the defensive strategy of managing expectations is a potent practice. Five-Star Bosses understand that in order to satisfy competing stakeholders, they must educate others to avoid unreliable assumptions and unrealistic forecasts.

Let's start with a simple business example. You go to a restaurant and there seem to be plenty of tables available, so after the host seats you, you look through the menu and quickly decide what you want. But as you wait, you look at your watch and realize you have a meeting coming up and no one has come to take your order. You try to flag down staff members who seem to ignore your raised hand, and your frustration begins to rise. After a few more minutes, you walk back up to the host and explain that you're in a hurry and no one has come to take your order after several minutes. The host then says, "Oh, I'm so sorry, the wait person in your area had an accident and the manager is taking her to the hospital. I'll make sure someone comes right over."

So while the new information doesn't change your need to order your food, the extra info gives you an entirely different attitude. Now you feel empathy for the wait person and can appreciate the staffing shortage in the restaurant. A proactive host person, boss, or other wait person could have come to your table and noted an emergency and a plea for patience. Sometimes, those simple extended messages make all the difference between a happy customer and an irate one. That's why it's important to manage expectations.

A good part of your role, even though it will probably never be on your job description, is to help people above you, below you, and beside you stay informed as to progress, timelines, and budget issues. Humans, by nature, are goal-striving beings. We have a sense of what we want, whether it's food, pay, or how others should respond to us. When there is a gap between what a person expects and what they get, this creates tension. Regardless of how realistic these expectations are, people get frustrated, irritated, and eventually angry when the gap grows. The longer it took for you to get waited on at the restaurant, the larger the gap became.

Five-Star Bosses understand the concept of these gaps, so that you can decrease tension among stakeholders you work with as well as preserve your reputation as a person who gets things done. A boss who adjusts expectations is perceived much stronger than one who does not, even if the actual work product is the same. Managing expectations is generally a communication issue, in that informed people have less of a gap between what they expect and what they experience. In the restaurant example, the host missed an opportunity to close the gap by simply letting you know when she was seating you that they were temporarily down a couple of people on the floor. This empowered you to leave, sit at the bar, or just lower your time assumptions.

Often you'll hear how the stock price of a company declines on the market when anticipated quarterly goals are not met. Nothing in that announcement changed the value of the company, but the fact that there was a gap between what was expected and what was reported caused people to lower their sense of value in the stock's worth. Sometimes, the best performers aren't the ones who achieve more; they're the ones who manage expectations best. Someone said, "I have no goals, therefore I'm never disappointed when I don't achieve anything." I'm certainly not suggesting that, but I am saying that staying ahead of the game in terms of managing these spoken and unspoken assumptions will save you a lot of grief and frustration among those you serve.

Discerning Expectations

At the time of writing this book, I'm 60 years old. Fortunately, I've never had to wear glasses throughout my life. But in the last few years, I do need reading glasses for smaller print as in books and many restaurant menus. I can increase the font size on laptops and cell phones, but having those magnifier lenses helps a lot by increasing clarity and reducing eye strain. Most expectations are blurry. Therefore, part of your job is to be the reading glasses for your boss and your team members. Sometimes expectations are very clear, but more frequently they are not. "Get your job done" is somewhat vague. "I need the complete report emailed to me by 5pm on Friday" is clear. Naturally, context dictates the clarity in terms of what's expected and how your organization operates, but most of the time, you'll need to bring focus.

Sometimes it's as simple as providing a SMART goal for your team and asking for the SMART goal from your supervisor (specific, measurable, attainable, relevant, timely). Managing expectations is a dance. When you're new in your role, you'll need to be more intentional than after you've become more familiar with the role. But if your supervisor or a team member is new, then you need to treat the situation as if you're new. Never assume they'll understand. The old adage "When you assume, it makes an ass out of you and me" is very true when it comes to expectations. Implicit leadership is the unwritten, internal assumptions we have about how a leader should behave. As I've mentioned, this is why so many people have differing opinions on a leader, because they look at leaders through their lenses. These are assumed expectations. When we fail to communicate what we expect, then we run the risk of failing. Just because it is clear to you, you can't assume it's clear to others. Let's look at the differences of this when you're the boss and when you're the direct report.

Expectations Wisdom

"Peace begins when expectation ends." -Sri Chinmoy

"Expectation is the root of all heartache." - William Shakespeare

"Expectations are premeditated resentments." - Alcoholics Anonymous

"You can't expect your employees to exceed the expectations of your customers, if you don't exceed the employees' expectations of management." — Howard Schultz

"What screws us up most in life is the picture in our head of how it's supposed to be." — Anonymous

"Too many people miss the silver lining, because they were expecting gold." - Maurice Setter

Managing Up

Bosses have direct reports and are direct reports. We've discussed the dynamic tension of this, but it needs to be discussed further in the context of managing expectations, since this goes both ways but looks different for each. Like all bosses, your supervisor is on a scale of effectiveness and ineffectiveness. Some are very impatient and assume that direct reports should be able to read their minds, know what they want, and respond appropriately. They communicate poorly and then when their expectations aren't met, they melt down, yelling in person or over the phone or in email, acting as if everyone except them is incompetent and imbecilic. Don't be that boss to your team members. You're better than that. They deserve better than that.

Yet, if your boss is like that, then it's your job to be proactive and figure out what it is your boss wants. Although it is his job to let you know expectations, don't let his being a jerk demotivate you from doing your homework. "John, what specifically do you want from my team in this project? We want to make sure we meet your expectations, but it will help us to understand what would ring your bell." Put it in your own words. You get the gist. The point is to be specific. Take notes. The less specific it is, the greater the potential gap you're allowing for your boss to be disappointed. Chances are you don't want to ask how it should be done, because that's your job and you'll irritate your boss. He'll assume you're not a leader. But do ask for the outcome and the quality of the work product he's expecting.

The minor irritation this may provoke will be outweighed by conveying your desire to perform well and please your boss. Who doesn't like being pleased? Don't keep coming back for minuscule, play-by-play details, unless that's what he wants. Get a strong sense of what is expected and then only come back if you discover that during the project, you won't be able to deliver when or how it was articulated. That's a part of managing expectations. If the report was due Friday at 5pm but there's a hiccup in the supply chain preventing you from delivering on time, then if there's no way you can fix it, let your boss know ASAP. If you tell him at 5pm that it won't be in on time because of the supplier, it will make you look bad. Obviously, if you get the report to him by 5pm on Thursday, it makes you look better than merely meeting the deadline. Little instances like this tend to accumulate, so that we get judged according to our ability to match expectations. Thus, when these need to be adjusted, that's a part of our job as well. Keeping your boss in the loop is important. If you have a micro-managing boss, it's critical.

Managing Down

Do you want to be pleased by your team? Then let them know how you operate. What are your expectations? Chances are, they want to please you. Don't leave them guessing. The more you do that, the greater your stress and theirs. Articulate what is important to you. Do you prefer email or face-to-face communication? Should they call or text you? Do you expect them to be in their office by a specific time, or is it flexible? Do you want to see the expense receipts, or is it okay just to hand them in to the bookkeeper? There are potentially dozens of issues related to your expectations, so the more you can articulate them and offer examples, the less chance you and your team will get frustrated.

One supervisor I know has an employee who interrupts her throughout the day when she's in her office, offering little updates on issues. After hearing about this irritation a few times, I asked, "Have you ever told her about how these interruptions keep you from being focused on tasks or if there's a better way for her to perform?" She answered, "No, I haven't. I don't want to demotivate her." This employee probably wants to keep her boss abreast of the issues or simply seeks her attention. I don't know because I've not asked her. So while this supervisor has great people skills, it is also an example of how Agreeableness can do a disservice to leading. She's allowing the employee to dig her own grave by not informing her of how the interruptions are irritating. She could say, "Ruby, I can tell that you want to keep me informed and I appreciate that. At the same time, I want to keep an open-door policy for all of our employees. Moving forward, it would really help me if you accumulated your reports and updates and then came to me only once or twice a day, so that I can concentrate on my other tasks more effectively. Could you do that for me?"

Naturally, it may take a few times for your direct reports to get a sense of what you expect in a variety of situations. That's okay, because over the long run, it will help everyone work more effectively and sleep better at night. When possible, be specific. This illustrates what your expectations look like in various settings. For example, instead of saying, "Let me know if any of our customers aren't getting their products on time," you might say, "For example, if ABC company calls and says they've not gotten their order of parts, take care of it but also make sure you send me an email within an hour so that I can see how many times this is happening. Is that expectation clear?" The more exact you can be, the better. Chances are you've worked for a boss who always left you guessing what it was he wanted from his employees. Figuring that out could be a painful process, with people whispering among themselves, trying to figure out what they thought he really wanted.

Managing Laterally

Managing laterally refers to how you get along with colleagues at your level, bosses of other teams or divisions, and customers. Throughout history, companies have gotten into big trouble not because they made mistakes, but because they didn't warn the public or inform customers of potential issues when they discovered them. Naturally, everyone wants to preserve their reputation, but problems often escalate when we fail to manage expectations in advance and warn people of potential problems. So what does this mean? Well, in the case of the restaurant example, it may mean letting a customer know when losing a key player on your team that it may cause a longer wait time. It could be letting them know that an embargo in China on a specific product you need for your component means a delay in delivery. There are countless potential issues that can arise, but the bottom line is that whenever you can help another person modify his or her expectations appropriately, the happier that person will be once you meet those expectations. You're reducing the gap between what we hope for and what we get.

Certainly we can't always remove gaps, but reducing them is sometimes all it takes. If it's going to take three days to fix the car, don't tell them two days. It's better to say four days and deliver it one day early, because you're establishing a more realistic expectation. When people overestimate what they can do in hopes of getting someone's business, they set themselves up for failure. People are a lot more open to the truth than we often believe. Eventually, your reputation as a straight shooter will win you the respect of your colleagues, customers, and those you serve.

What we've been talking about here is related to hope. Hope is the state of mind that good things will happen, a preferred future where we'll experience what we desire. At the end of the day, your job as a Five-Star Boss is to fulfill hopes. When you fail to do this, people will be disappointed and your stock value will decrease. Expectations are little more than hopes wrapped up in actions and outcomes. So while you may want to perform well in your role, much of what you do is based on fulfilling people emotionally. Managing expectations is about increasing the level of hope in people by reducing the gap between what is expected and what is realized. Keeping this in mind on a daily basis will improve the likelihood that people will see you as a Five-Star Boss.

Five-Star Boss Questions:

1. What is an aha you got from this chapter?
2. Describe an example of where you failed to meet another's expectations.
3. If you could do it over, what would you change? How could you manage expectations better?
4. What do you need to do to improve in this area with your boss?
5. What can you do to improve with your direct reports?

Chapter 25

Work-Life Balance Myth

Living in the Tension

Busyness vs. Hurriedness

Have you ever noticed that hardly anyone is too busy to tell you how busy they are? Ask nearly any person, "How are you doing?" and you'll hear some version of, "Oh, I'm so busy." It's become such a trite reply that my wife and I made a pact never to respond that way when people ask. Everyone seems busy. The area where we live has a lot of retired people who no longer work, yet many of them say, "I've never been busier." Oh brother! Here's the deal: busyness is the new normal, so how do you keep your work as a manager from sucking the life out of you? Research shows that people feel more stressed at work than ever, yet annually, 25-40% of vacation days go unused. Perhaps there's a correlation. I understand the challenges of getting away and the fear that while you're gone things will fall apart. And then there's all the part-timing that goes on, whether it's a side-business, 2nd job, or merely family responsibilities with school, sports, and more.

Most of the time, when you become a boss, it means you'll be putting in longer hours than before you were in charge. You'll recognize the back of your team members' heads as they walk out of the office to the parking lot, while you're plucking away at piles of emails and reports.

One of the books I used in my Human Capital Performance and Motivation course at USC was *Great at Work: How Top Performers Do Less, Work Better, and Achieve More* by UC Berkley professor Morten Hansen. I recommend it if you want research-based ideas to work more effectively, beyond basic time management techniques, worthy as they are. Usually, those in supervisory roles have more to do than when they were technical specialists. One reason is that most companies consider salaried people as on the clock, regardless of the hour. Another reason is that there's always something else you could be doing. In addition to all the managerial tasks, such as meetings, paperwork, and preparing reports, you have leadership tasks such as strategic planning, developing staff, and interacting with your team.

But what's the difference between busyness and hurriedness? A friend of mine pointed out that busyness isn't bad, so long as you're productive, getting your work done, and having a sense of accomplishment. Hurriedness, on the other hand, is more about the nagging feeling that you never have enough time, what you're doing isn't making much difference, and you can't find satisfaction. Busyness comes and goes. Hurriedness tends to linger with us, like a nagging headache or driving in the fog at night. It's more of a state of mind that infiltrates our well-being and thus our effectiveness as a boss.

The emerging workforce is more likely to value work/life balance than the preceding ones. This isn't a sign that they're lazy, just that they have priorities in addition to work. Many saw the results of missing parents growing up, and so they want to find more purpose in life than work. That means figuring out how to get things done at work more efficiently and effectively than in the past, when people were more prone to come in earlier and stay later. This is in addition to your own life as a boss. The last thing you want to come home to after a long day at work is a resentful spouse and kids who feel neglected. Family and friends are great energy replenishers, so long as they feel loved. When they're not, we're like a sinking ship taking on even more water.

Leaning In

During my mid-30s, I was finishing my doctorate, working on a book, and leading a capital campaign for a non-profit I led, not to mention my wife and I having three young sons at home. I began feeling tired, and there seemed to be a sort of lump in my throat when I swallowed. My mind raced to the possibility of cancer. While sitting in a doctor's office, the physician asked, "Have you been under any stress lately?" I said, "Not really." Immediately my wife interjected, "What do you mean? Of course you have." The doc suggested I slow down my pace for a while. Sure enough, my energy returned and I lost the lump feeling in my throat.

There are numerous books and resources related to work/life balance, but here are five observations I've gleaned from my 40-plus years of work life and from coaching numerous leaders. I challenge you to lean into them, along with creating your own set of norms for living.

#1. Discern the seasons. In Scottsdale, Arizona, we used to joke about the four seasons being early summer, summer, late summer, and next summer. But I grew up in the Midwest where we had four very distinct seasons: winter, spring, summer, fall. Living on a farm, we had specific practices, clothes, and work based on the season. Work and life also come in seasons, although not as predictably as on the calendar. During busy work seasons, you need to put in extra time and effort or, as we

said in Iowa, "make hay when the sun's shining." There also come times when work is less demanding. Take advantage of these to let up, inhale, and recharge your batteries. Recognize the ebb and flow; bear down, let up; push hard, relax. Get good at hearing the beat of life's rhythm and get in sync with it.

#2. Relationships are like plants. Even though I grew up on a farm, I don't have a green thumb. Although we now have a patio with plants that I fertilize and water consistently, most of my adult life consisted of buying a plant and then tossing out its leafy carcass in a few weeks. That's why the inside of our house only has silk plants. Plants need water, sunshine, and fertilizer. Relationships have a life of their own, therefore they need nutrients to grow as well. Five-Star Bosses nurture their important relationships. If your superior never asks for a meeting, then you ask him. If your direct reports haven't been in touch with you lately, then you contact them. Who is in your network with whom you need to connect? Sending an email, text, or leaving a voicemail are all ways of cultivating your key relationships. Like plants, they won't survive if you ignore them.

#3. Embrace the race. Steve Jobs, the visionary founder of Apple, stated his life purpose was to make a dent in the universe. Philosophers and spiritual leaders throughout history have helped people connect their work with divine, higher order purposes. While clergy often emphasize their calling, referring to the voice of God telling them to enter the ministry, sometimes the rest of us feel overlooked. But the word "vocation" is derived from the Latin term *vocare*, or to call. Thus, a person's vocation is God's voice or call for one's life. Although you may not be in your dream job yet, it allows you to put food on the table, care for your loved ones, and is a way to serve others.

A few years ago, I taught a course for the Naval Postgraduate School in a program for Army accountants titled Army Cost Warriors. The theme helped people far removed from the tip of the spear to understand how their effectiveness impacted the lives of frontline warriors. With overspending and wasteful practices, there may not be money available to purchase the Kevlar vests that could save the lives of soldiers in battle. This offered inspiration for "bean counters" to understand their role in the big picture. "Embrace the race" means to accept that. While work is difficult and demanding, it's what you're called to do.

#4. Life is triune. Our lives consist of three primary spheres: physical, mental, and spiritual. These overlap more than most realize. When we are physically healthy, we're far more apt to feel alive emotionally and socially. Good nutrition and exercise are good for the head, not just the heart and lungs. If you want to be a peak performer and not just peek at performing, nurture each of these areas. The Greek word for soul is the basis of the word "psychology." These intermingle, so whether your spirituality involves a faith, religious activities, or simply meditation and prayer, practice these. When you're emotionally upset, it's difficult to think straight, and you get knots in your gut. That's because these spheres intertwine. Pull on one, and the others move. Homeostasis is a state of balance and integration. When your body is in homeostasis, its systems are in sync with each other. Staying healthy in each of your three spheres is important for handling stress well.

#5. Keep it real. The emerging workforce, born between 1980-2000 and commonly referred to as millennials, seem to appreciate authenticity more than previous generations. Reality TV, social media, and any number of get-real movements such as #MeToo are making us rethink how we live. Large retailing chains now reject ads selling cosmetics using airbrushed, photo-shopped models. At the end of the day, people seek authenticity. So while I understand that as a boss, we feel the pressure to look good, perform well, and keep up our guard, it's okay to keep it real. People are interested in role models, everyday heroes who admit that they wrestle with competing priorities. As a leader, people look at you for cues. One thing you can offer your team that you won't find in your job description is modeling how to do life as an employee, family person, and citizen of the world. Empathy, along with sharing your own struggles and failure where appropriate, are ways to reduce your stress as well as win the respect of others. Keeping up appearances

is emotionally taxing, costing you unnecessary loss of energy.

What the SEALs Taught Me

What we do away from the job affects what we do on the job. In 2015, I was on a team of people looking into the dynamic changes if women began serving as Navy SEALs. That's because in 2016, new policies in the military stated that women could try out for any role, including special forces. Until that time, females could not apply. I went to Coronado, where BUD/S training is conducted, to interview SEALs and those who work with them. Some of the natural concerns involved physical strength, wear and tear, and in the case of a pregnancy, losing a vital team member and disrupting significant practice, jeopardizing a mission. Special forces often embed in remote areas while they wait for strategic conditions as well as to do work-ups, the term given to rehearsing an assault. What I wasn't expecting to hear was concern for spouses and partners back home, wondering what might be happening in a high-octane, co-ed SEAL team. In essence, they were more concerned with how their family members' anxiety might draw energy from the mission, more than any temptation from the situation itself.

The point is that family life issues do impact work conditions, real and perceived. When someone is going through a health scare or legal issue, is experiencing marital or parenting problems, these deter a person from being as effective on the job. Time away, distractions, calls and emails, and interruptions in meetings must be handled when you're the person in charge. Caring for yourself as well as your people can be more burdensome than work itself. In my wife's industry, senior care, research shows that spouses caring for loved ones often have shorter life spans than the ones with dementia, because of the added stress. Consulting with a counselor, relying on close friends, and communicating appropriately with each other as a team are important ways that members can manage difficult times. Pretending everything is fine and ignoring the elephant in the room often make things worse. Compartmentalizing our lives does not work over the long haul.

Proper Tension

Think of your life as a violin string. A master violinist listens to the tension in her instrument's strings. Too little, and notes are flat. Too much, and notes are sharp. Five-Star Bosses learn to hear the pitch in their lives, balancing the too little and too much tension. The only tension-free state is death. Living in the tension means you're alive. Hearing the tones suggest time off are as much a part of workplace effectiveness as knowing when to push harder. As someone said, "No one ever said on their death bed, 'You know, I wish I'd put in more time at the office.'" People do confess the other, though. Recognize that most leaders consistently feel the tension between professional and personal life. Familiarity with it won't make it disappear.

Five-Star Boss Questions:

1. How would you differentiate busyness from hurriedness?
2. What areas do you struggle with the most In work/life balance?
3. Describe a time when you seemed to be in a great time of balance. What were the conditions surrounding this time?
4. Which of the five Leaning In ideas did you find most beneficial? Why do you think that?
5. Which of the three primary spheres (physical, mental, spiritual) need the most focus right now in your life? What can you do about this?

Chapter 26

Quick Picks

Best-Practice Ideas You'll Find Helpful

But Wait, There's More

Following are an array of ideas that didn't warrant entire chapters, but reflect skills related to being a Five-Star Boss. Following that is a section of survey responses from people asked about weaknesses of bosses they've had. This sort of raw content can serve as a way for you to measure your impact and learn what to avoid. The chapter wraps up with 10 classic leadership articles and 10 classic leadership book recommendations to expand your development toward becoming a Five-Star Boss.

- **LinkedIn:** Everyone interested in developing a professional network should have a LinkedIn account. Some of my military, government, and public service students don't see the need for this, but it makes sense as business cards fade into oblivion and people want to know a bit more about you. Consider this a personal website where you brand yourself. You have a brand, whether you realize it or not. A LinkedIn account lets you take more control of how people perceive you. Expand your network with others in your industry, where you plan to hire, or where you'll eventually migrate. Use a professional photo and take advantage of content to expand your learning. Many members post great articles, videos, and blogs. Even those you follow reflect your personal brand and interests. Plus, for a modest fee, you can subscribe to LinkedIn Learning, a huge library of video training on a variety of subjects.

- **Social Media:** By now, given all the scandals we've heard in the news the last several years, hopefully you realize the potential danger in what you post on social media. Comments, photos, who you follow, Likes, and what you post can come back to haunt you and is difficult to remove, once it's on the internet. Between 50% and 70% of bosses and HR people perform internet searches on their job candidates. A growing number of current employers periodically check the internet for employees, especially those with more influence who could potentially embarrass an organization. What happens in Vegas no longer stays in Vegas.

- **The Raise**: Most companies have written protocol regarding salaries and raises. You'll want to find out more about how your organization handles these. The general rule is to ask what you can at the start, since this becomes the basis for future raises. Although they'll offer a specific amount, most companies have a range in order to retain room for negotiating up at the start. By the time they offer you the job, they want you, so it's the best time to negotiate. Keep in mind a 5% raise on $60K is $3K, but the same increase on $70K is $3.5K. Know your industry standards before you get to the final offer. Check online sources such as Glassdoor, and figure in your experience and the cost of living in your area. For example, it costs a lot more to live in Los Angeles than in Kansas City. Also, unless your company has scheduled pay adjustments every 6 to 12 months, make sure you initiate this with your supervisor at least once a year.

- **They Own You**: Legally, most companies own everything you do at work and on company equipment, such as computers, tablets, cell phones, networks, and corporate internet. You may be familiar with these guidelines, but if you're new to the organization, this is a friendly reminder. Unless you have a contractual exception, they have dibs on your IP (intellectual property) if it's created during work or on company equipment. The same is true of your communication. As your influence grows in your company, the more weight is placed on what you say, how you say it, and where you go. Because of increasing scrutiny on management, companies are concerned about public relation firestorms. While most don't, companies can review everything you say and send on company emails, whether or not it's on your computer. Text and travel records become court case evidence if there's a legal concern. A general rule of thumb is to assume everything you say and send will be plastered on a freeway billboard near you. If you'd be embarrassed to see it there with your name, don't say it or send it.

- **Feed-forward NOT Feedback:** One of the most powerful skills for developing your team members is to offer suggestions for improvement based on the future, not the past. Feedback suggests what the person did well and did not do well. The problem with feedback is that you can't change the past. This results in regret and hopelessness, because none of us can undo history. A more hopeful and proactive approach is to place your input in future tense instead of past tense. Napoleon said that "leaders are purveyors of hope." When you say, "Ben, you should have put your concern on the agenda," you're focusing on the past. A more effective way of saying the same thing is, "Ben, next time you'll be even more effective if you put your concern on the agenda so we are prepared to discuss it." Note that the rearview mirror in your car is much smaller than the windshield. Looking back has its place, but the future is ahead, so focus there.

- **MBWA**: Every manager has a unique style, but a practice of Five-Star Bosses is that they manage by wandering around (MBWA). Bosses feel burdened with increased meetings, added report preparation, and managerial responsibilities. They're tempted to spend more time in their offices, secluded from what's going on in the floor and among their direct reports. Don't do it. Your new mantra is "I'm in the people business." Therefore, you need to see and be seen. A pastor friend and I were talking after church one time and he graciously interrupted our conversation. "Well, I need to go slap some backs and kiss some babies." He joked about the practice, but genuinely enjoyed people. Five-Star Bosses are visible among their people and make sure they are present in strategic times. For example, my wife knows that in her work, senior residents gather for meals. Therefore, she makes a point to visit her "customers" when they're together, to increase the number of visits in a short amount of time and be seen doing this.

- **Never Bad-Mouth Your Boss:** Sometimes, managers fall prey to one of the oldest traps in organizational life: complaining about their boss to their direct reports. The temptation of this cheap therapy is to endear yourself to your workers, especially if you disagree with a policy or practice employed by your superior. There are three primary reasons to avoid this. First, it sets a poor role model and establishes a standard that it's okay to complain about your boss. Think about it; you're their boss, so if you criticize yours, they're more apt to do the same to you. Second, it undermines your company and in turn lowers your value. If a company approves the practices of a person in management by placing him there, then by devaluing your boss, you decrease your own worth. Defacing someone else's furniture doesn't make yours any prettier. Third, you never know when word will get out that you maligned your boss. You can't control feedback loops, so you're taking a risk. If you don't say anything, chances are slim they'll make up content. Five-Star Bosses display integrity by not bad-mouthing their bosses to others.

- **What Goals Trump Performance Goals:** In Chapter 14 on motivation principles, we discussed goal setting. Research shows that people are motivated by challenging goals except when the person lacks skills to accomplish them. In these situations, managers should set learning goals. For example, let's say you have a new employee who has never done sales, but now it's her primary task. Eventually you may want to set quotas, but without a proficiency, she'll quickly feel defeated and highly demotivated. A learning goal may involve a certain amount of time spent in sales training webinars, being mentored by a top seller, or any number of other milestones based on learning how to sell, not actual sales. Once learning goals are met, sales quota goals will then motivate the employee, assuming they're reachable.

- **Executive Disease**: Do you know what Executive Disease is? Now that you're a part of management, you should. It's living in the "boss bubble." When you become a boss, you'll no longer receive the same type of communication and feedback that you did when you were a team member. Sure, you'll know more about your organization than your direct reports, but from now on, people will edit what they say and how they say it. That means to a certain extent, you'll be in the dark. Most leaders think they're doing better than their people think they are. Because you possess authoritative (positional) power, people aren't going to be as honest as they were when you were one of them. This bubble means that while you think you'll be in the know, bosses hear an altered reality modified by those who don't want to be honest for fear of being demoted, alienated, or considered a snitch by peers. Be aware of executive disease and do your best to remedy it, although you'll never be fully cured.

Who's Your Boss?

As a boss, do you know who your boss is? Actually, it's your customers. But who are they? Your *primary* customers are your superior and your direct reports. That's right, your job is to serve the people on your team by leading them well. This serves them and your supervisor. If you do that, they will take care of your larger customer base. Here is an array of comments representative of thousands of conversations I've had and responses I've received when I asked people about their boss irritations. These are in their words. This offers insights to fix the Executive Disease mentioned above. Which of these might your people say about you? And if you don't think they'd say it about you, how do you know they wouldn't?

- Biggest weakness is a lack of leadership skills. New managers need to know how to take care of people. Bosses fail to develop their personnel.

- They need to trust their team and not micromanage. Not everything will be a life-or-death situation. They need to assess a situation properly and respond appropriately. Short-term setbacks are okay if it means success later on.

- Lack of helping and motivating the employees.

- Knowing the boundaries of their authority, but using that authority and willingness to lead.

- Failure to adapt their management style to suit individuals under their area of responsibility.

- Over-bossing others around. Not giving employees enough room to grow and make mistakes. Trusting in the employees' abilities.

- New managers often try to jump in and make changes without learning what their employees do on a daily basis, the dynamics of the team, their strengths and weaknesses, etc. I feel that if they put themselves in a "trial" run to learn the ins and outs of their new team before implementing change, it would be better received by the team.

- Implementing change too early without fully understanding the status quo.

- Weakness: Tries to make everyone happy instead of disciplining those that need it. What they need to know the most: Everyone has a weakness, but they also have strengths. Build on both by pairing them with someone with the opposite so they can feed from each other, at an early point in their career, and throughout thereafter. Bosses fail by not keeping the mid-level leaders involved in major changes. My leaders kept me in the dark as they were planning to move my people to other areas. I seriously resent that and have serious disrespect for said management.

- Ability to see the unique factors that can motivate different individuals. Show of empathy. Assuming that all staff are as competent as them or accepting differing views from theirs.

- I have a new manager personally. He is still in a technical mindset rather than focusing on leading his new team. The team feels a lack of support.

- Forgetting where they came from and where they used to be. Some managers are "too ready" to step into their new role that they forget to put themselves into shoes of staff.

- The biggest weakness of new managers is not understanding their employees and not understanding how things should be done so that everyone works together. Managers need to know how to help others and work with them instead of letting them fail. New bosses fail when they struggle to ask for help and look to others who need help. New managers also struggle to adjust to how a new company does things.

- Micromanagement and lack of trust.

- They don't have soft skills; fail to get to know their people; fail to develop relationships/trust and lead by example.

- A manager or leader that infrequently and inconsistently shares information that impacts the team is a big weakness. Additionally, micro-managers tend to fail because they do not build trust in their team.

- A weakness of new managers is changing the organization in ways that harm processes that were not broken. Their style may not be the best fit in all categories of a workplace. Fix what's broken, but keep what works. A workplace runs on people. We need to put our people first and learn how to leverage their strengths so that the full team succeeds. Bosses fail when they do not understand the value an employee brings. Some employees need to fail in order to learn, others need direction in order to succeed. Leadership needs to be applied to the individual level so that we can shape the workforce we have into the workforce we want.

- Biggest weakness. Not getting to know your employees at the individual level. What motivates them and inspires them. Bosses need to provide consistency in delivery of their direction and how to explain changes as change is constant. Where bosses fail is addressing personnel issues. Need to address issues when they come up and not wait for the 10th time.

- Not trusting and empowering their team.

- New managers often struggle with finding a voice - one to lead the team, represent the team, defend the team, champion innovative ideas on behalf of the team. A supervisor who says he/she wants innovative ideas and then won't take them to upper management with conviction and dedication to the idea will often get shut down at the higher level. This means that the idea will never take flight, and after a while, the team will become discouraged and stop providing the ideas in the first place, and, worse, the team will become cynical about what management say they want (words without follow-through).

- Being able to relate to their subordinates.

- Already having an idea how they're going to run their team without understanding the climate in the workforce first.

- Being afraid/too insecure to make decisions.

- Biggest weakness - lack of interpersonal aptitude: the inability to understand what motivates team members and how to promote collaboration.

- Biggest weakness of new managers is thinking you are the most important or smartest person. Learning how to empower and leverage the team is the art of management.

- Managers fail because they lack good communication skills. Their inability to be transparent and keep their employees abreast of what is going on can lead to a culture of rumors and misguided information circulating in a workplace. Managers fail because they do not show appreciation to their employees. Many managers are more focused on their own career and being recognized that they do not take ample time to say "Thank You" or put their team in for awards or establish a system to recognize achievements.

- In both the military and the civilian workplace, the biggest weakness that I have seen is new managers failing to heed the advice of the senior staff. They have valuable experience, and listening to their process / reasoning can be valuable, even if it needs to be updated.

- Micro-managing an experienced team that probably knows more than the new supervisor. Read the room, ask questions, LISTEN & get to know the team before professing to be their leader. A good LEADER is also a good FOLLOWER.

THE FIVE-STAR BOSS

CareerBuilder.com Survey*

Although this survey was done nearly a decade ago, chances are it reflects what is true for today, since little research exists to suggest anything different. Following are results from a survey of over 2400 employers and 3900 workers in the U.S.

> When it comes to rating their direct supervisor, 20 percent described their direct supervisor's performance as poor or very poor. The top concerns workers have with their boss include:

- Plays favorites – 23 percent
- Doesn't follow through on what he/she promises – 21 percent
- Doesn't listen to concerns – 21 percent
- Doesn't provide regular feedback – 20 percent
- Doesn't motivate me – 17 percent
- Only provides negative feedback – 14 percent

> When it comes to rating the performance of their corporate leaders, 23 percent described their performance as poor or very poor. Corporate leaders received a poor rating from workers primarily due to insufficient communication, unrealistic workloads, and a lack or training and employee development:

- Doesn't make an effort to listen to employees or address employee morale – 40 percent
- Not enough transparency, doesn't communicate openly and honestly – 33 percent
- Major changes are made without warning – 30 percent
- Workloads and productivity demands are unreasonable – 27 percent
- Doesn't motivate me – 21 percent
- Stopped investing in the development of employees – 20 percent

Top Reading Suggestions From the Author

10 Classic Leadership Books: (Note: *I once had over 700 books on leadership in my personal library. When people ask me what leadership books I recommend, I tell them it depends on where they're at in their growth and leadership journey. Since I don't know you personally, I'm offering this list of "can't miss" classics you'll appreciate.* -Alan)

> *The 21 Irrefutable Laws of Leadership* by John C. Maxwell, 1998, Thomas Nelson Pub. (A street-smart guide from my previous mentor.)
>
> *Primal Leadership* by Daniel Goleman, Richard Boyatzis, and Annie McKee, 2002, Harvard Business School Press. (Focuses on emotional intelligence in the context of leading.)
>
> *Leading Change* by John P. Kotter, 1996, Harvard Business School Press. (A great, eight-step model that is research-based, focusing on effective org change.)
>
> *Leadership Is an Art* by Max DePree, 1989, Random House. (An easy read by the former CEO of Herman-Miller, focusing on what it means to lead.)

The One Minute Manager by Ken Blanchard & Spencer Johnson, 1982, Simon & Schuster. (This bestseller put Ken Blanchard on the leadership gurus list; an easy read in narrative format.)

Servant Leadership by Robert Greenleaf, 1977, Paulist Press. (A servant leader must first learn how to serve. This book is the Bible of leader-as-servant.)

The Five Dysfunctions of a Team by Patrick Lencioni, 2002, Jossey-Bass. (Anyone who leads a team needs to know how they can go bad, to help them get good.)

On Leadership by John Gardner, 1990, Free Press. (While more thoughtful, Gardner offers amazing insights into the world of leading.)

On Becoming a Leader by Warren Bennis, 2009, Basic Books. (Bennis, a former USC professor, hit a homerun with this great read.)

The Leadership Challenge by James Kouzes & Barry Posner, 2007, Jossey-Bass. (This book offers an array of practical ideas and some workbooks and tools to improve your leading.)

10 Classic Articles to Read:

"Eight Ways to Build Collaborative Teams" by L. Gratton & T. Erickson. Harvard Business Review, November, 2007.

"What Leaders Really Do" by John Kotter. Harvard Business Review, December, 2001.

"Let's Hear It for B Players" by Thomas DeLong and Vineeta Vijayaraghavan, Harvard Business Review, June, 2003.

"Managers and Leaders: Are They Different?" by Abraham Zaleznik. Harvard Business Review, January, 2004.

"The Necessary Art of Persuasion" by Jay Conger. Harvard Business Review, May-June, 1998.

"Why Should Anyone Be Led by You?" Robert Goffee & Gareth Jones. Harvard Business Review, Sept-Oct., 2000.

"What Great Managers Do" by Marcus Buckingham. Harvard Business Review, March, 2005.

"Level 5 Leadership" by Jim Collins. Harvard Business Review, January, 2001.

"What Makes an Effective Executive" by Peter Drucker. Harvard Business Review, June, 2004.

"Discovering Your Authentic Leadership" by Bill George, Peter Sims, Andrew N. McLean & Diana Mayer. Harvard Business Review, February, 2007.

FIVE STAR BOSS

Check out Dr. Nelson's podcast series that supplements content in this book, without replicating it. These are free. Most are in 5-minute formats and are downloadable: https://thenelsons.podbean.com/.

* The nationwide survey was conducted among more than 2,480 U.S. employers and 3,910 U.S. workers between November 15 and December 2, 2010. CareerBuilder.com

ABOUT THE AUTHOR

Alan E. Nelson is a leader, professor, and social entrepreneur. Most of his life he's led. After earning a doctorate in leadership from the University of San Diego, he began writing and teaching other leaders. Then at midlife he changed gears, focusing on identifying and developing leaders while they're most pliable, between the ages of 3 and 18. He's the founder of KidLead Inc. (non-profit) and LeadYoung Training Systems, making an impact internationally.

Alan teaches leadership, organizational behavior, and human capital performance and motivation courses at USC Marshall School of Business, the Naval Postgraduate School, and the University of California Irvine's Merage School of Business. He's the author of over 20 books and 100s of articles and podcasts, and he has designed an array of young leader training curricula.

Married to Nancy for over 38 years, the Nelsons have three grown sons and two wonderful granddaughters. They live in Thousand Oaks, California, just north of Los Angeles.

For more info on Alan and his speaking, go to www.AlanENelson.com or via LinkedIn. He's available for training on this book and related leadership topics. For info on his young leader resources, go to www.LeadYoungTraining.com.

In this engaging, fun-to-read narrative, Alan focuses on how to target the most important single relationship key: treating people with honor. When people behave in a dishonoring manner, it's usually an indicator of what's going on inside of them, not so much a reflection of others. Instead of reacting negatively, we can refocus our attention to address their real need, a desire to be valued.

The narrative takes place in various coffee shops in Monterey and Carmel, California, as the author interacts with a peculiar sage named Paul. It's an engaging story, but all the while explaining some of the most practical ideas to help you succeed in your relationships.

Available on Amazon.com

In this short, easy-to-read book, Dr. Nelson communicates very practical ways to make a difference in the lives of those we meet on a daily basis. In an intriguing story line, similar in style to *The Secret of People*, the author engages with a sage "tourist" visiting Malibu. The conversations and mysterious meetings result in discovering powerful insights for influencing others in five minutes or less. By recognizing these fertile, open windows, we can sow seeds of hope that in turn fulfill us as well. The busyness of life need not limit the impact we make with others.

This is a great book for families, organizations, and individuals who want to take advantage of increasing their impact in short bites.

Available on Amazon.com

Some of the most overlooked resources for leaders are handy tools for training others how to lead. This is not so much a book as it is a training manual, providing leaders and managers with 50 leadership lessons covering an array of sub-topics. Forty-five of the lessons include a 1-page handout (8x11 format) that can be copied for team members. There's also a 1-page Trainer section with suggestions on how to use the lesson, whether you have 5 or 35 minutes. The variety of topics allows you to select the ones that fit your situation, helping you train your team.

The final five lessons are discussion guides for movies with leadership themes. These make fun team-building opportunities but with a purpose. Various aspects of leading can be coached out via strategic questions, offered in the lessons.

Available on Amazon.com

The O Factor represents a significant amount of Dr. Nelson's research and work with emerging leaders, between the ages of 3-18, internationally. In it he looks at the role of genetics and ways to identify future leaders by observing behaviors in social settings. In addition, there are an array of practical suggestions for developing children, preteens and teens as leaders, designed for parents, educators and those who work with youth.

Available on Amazon.com